United States Government Accountability Office

Report to Congressional Committees

July 2012

FINANCIAL LITERACY

Overlap of Programs Suggests There May Be Opportunities for Consolidation

GAO

Accountability ★ Integrity ★ Reliability

GAO-12-588

July 2012

FINANCIAL LITERACY

Overlap of Programs Suggests There May Be Opportunities for Consolidation

Why GAO Did This Study

Financial literacy—the ability to use knowledge and skills to manage financial resources effectively—plays an important role in helping to ensure the financial health and stability of individuals and families. Federal agencies promote financial literacy through activities including print and online materials, broadcast media, individual counseling, and classroom instruction. In response to a mandate requiring GAO to identify duplicative government programs and activities, this report addresses (1) the cost of federal financial literacy activities; (2) the extent of their overlap and fragmentation; (3) the federal government's coordination of these activities; and (4) what is known about their effectiveness. GAO reviewed agency budget documents, strategic plans, performance reports, websites, and other materials, and interviewed representatives of federal agencies and other organizations.

What GAO Recommends

GAO recommends that CFPB clearly delineate with other agencies respective roles and responsibilities, and that the Financial Literacy and Education Commission identify options for consolidating federal financial literacy efforts and address the allocation of federal resources in its national strategy. CFPB neither agreed nor disagreed with these recommendations and the Department of the Treasury agreed with the recommendations directed to the commission.

View GAO-12-588. For more information, contact Alicia Puente Cackley at (202) 512-8678 or cackleya@gao.gov.

What GAO Found

The federal government spent about $68 million on 15 of the 16 financial literacy programs that were comprehensive in scope or scale in fiscal year 2010; cost data were not available for the Consumer Financial Protection Bureau (CFPB), which was created that year. In addition, about $137 million in federal funding in four other major programs was directed to housing counseling, which can include elements of financial education. Since fiscal year 2010, at least four of these programs have been defunded and CFPB has received resources to fund its financial literacy activities.

Federal financial literacy and housing counseling activities are spread across multiple agencies and programs. GAO has not identified duplication—programs providing the same activities and services to the same beneficiaries—but has found overlap—multiple programs with similar goals and activities—in areas such as housing counseling and the financial education of youth. Further, CFPB was charged with some financial education duties that overlap with those of other federal agencies, making it essential that their respective roles and responsibilities be clearly delineated to ensure efficient use of resources. Moreover, CFPB's creation may signal an opportunity for consolidating some federal financial literacy efforts, which would be consistent with federal goals of reorganizing and consolidating federal agencies to reduce the number of overlapping government programs.

Federal agencies have made progress in recent years in coordinating their financial literacy activities and collaborating with nonfederal entities, in large part due to the efforts of the federal multiagency Financial Literacy and Education Commission. The commission's 2011 national strategy includes some useful elements—such as plans to coordinate interagency communication, improve strategic partnerships, and promote evaluation. However, it does not recommend or provide guidance on the appropriate allocation of federal resources among programs and agencies, which GAO has found to be desirable in a national strategy. While the commission's governance structure presents challenges in addressing resource issues, without a clear discussion of resource needs and where resources should be targeted, policymakers lack information to help direct the strategy's implementation and help ensure efficient use of funds.

The wide range of federal financial literacy activities and evaluation methods makes it difficult to systematically assess overall effectiveness or compare results across programs. Among the federal financial literacy programs that we reviewed, most included some evaluation component. Some measured the effect on participant behavior and others assessed changes in participant knowledge or tracked output measures, such as the number of consumers reached. Rigorous evaluation measuring behavior change is costly and methodologically challenging and may not be practical for all types of activities. However, CFPB and other federal entities have new efforts under way that seek to determine the most effective approaches and programs, which GAO believes to be positive steps toward helping ensure the best and most efficient use of federal financial literacy resources.

Contents

Abbreviations

CFPB	Consumer Financial Protection Bureau
DOD	Department of Defense
Dodd-Frank Act	Dodd-Frank Wall Street Reform and Consumer Protection Act
FDIC	Federal Deposit Insurance Corporation
FTC	Federal Trade Commission
HUD	Department of Housing and Urban Development
SEC	Securities and Exchange Commission
Treasury	Department of the Treasury

United States Government Accountability Office
Washington, DC 20548

July 23, 2012

The Honorable Tim Johnson
Chairman
The Honorable Richard C. Shelby
Ranking Member
Committee on Banking, Housing, and Urban Affairs
United States Senate

The Honorable Spencer Bachus
Chairman
The Honorable Barney Frank
Ranking Member
Committee on Financial Services
House of Representatives

Financial literacy plays an important role in helping to ensure the financial health and stability of individuals and families, and economic and demographic changes in recent years have further highlighted the need to empower all Americans to make informed financial decisions. The federal government has played a key role in addressing financial literacy, and this role has evolved in recent years, particularly with the creation of the Financial Literacy and Education Commission in 2003 and the Bureau of Consumer Financial Protection, commonly referred to as the Consumer Financial Protection Bureau (CFPB), in 2010. At the same time, however, increasing fiscal constraints at government agencies, particularly with regard to discretionary spending, may limit the resources available for financial literacy efforts, underscoring the need for the most efficient use of these resources.

We have issued a series of reports on potential duplication, overlap, and fragmentation among federal programs, which have included information about financial literacy programs.[1] This report expands on these themes and addresses (1) what is known about the cost of federal financial literacy activities; (2) the extent and consequences of overlap and fragmentation among federal financial literacy activities; (3) what the federal government is doing to coordinate its financial literacy activities; and (4) what is known about the effectiveness of federal financial literacy activities.

To address the first objective, we collected cost information from congressional appropriations, agency budget justifications, and other sources as available. Where costs related to financial literacy were not discrete or clearly apparent from these documents, we worked with agency staff to develop cost estimates. To address the other objectives, we reviewed and analyzed relevant reports and surveys and federal agency strategic plans, performance and accountability reports, websites, budget justifications, performance data, and evaluations related to federal financial literacy efforts. We also interviewed staff of 17 federal agencies that we had identified in prior work as potentially having significant involvement in financial literacy, as well as staff of nonprofit organizations. A more extensive discussion of our scope and methodology appears in appendix I.

We conducted this performance audit from May 2011 to July 2012 in accordance with generally accepted government auditing standards. Those standards require that we plan and perform the audit to obtain sufficient, appropriate evidence to provide a reasonable basis for our findings and conclusions based on our audit objectives. We believe that the evidence obtained provides a reasonable basis for our findings and conclusions based on our audit objectives.

---

[1]Public Law 111-139 required us to identify and report annually on federal programs, agencies, offices, and initiatives, either within departments or governmentwide, which have duplicative goals or activities. Pub. L. No. 111-139, § 21, 124 Stat. 29 (2010), 31 U.S.C. § 712 Note. For recent GAO work on potential duplication, overlap, and fragmentation among federal financial literacy programs, see GAO, *2012 Annual Report: Opportunities to Reduce Duplication, Overlap and Fragmentation, Achieve Savings, and Enhance Revenue*, GAO-12-342SP (Washington, D.C.: Feb. 28, 2012), pp. 151-154; *Follow-up on 2011 Report: Status of Actions Taken to Reduce Duplication, Overlap, and Fragmentation, Save Tax Dollars, and Enhance Revenue*, GAO-12-453SP (Washington, D.C.: Feb. 28, 2012), pp. 53-54; and *Opportunities to Reduce Potential Duplication in Government Programs, Save Tax Dollars, and Enhance Revenue*, GAO-11-318SP (Washington, D.C.: Mar. 1, 2011).

Background

Financial literacy, which is sometimes also referred to as financial capability, has been defined as the ability to use knowledge and skills to manage financial resources effectively for a lifetime of well-being. Financial literacy encompasses financial education—the process whereby individuals improve their knowledge and understanding of financial products, services, and concepts. However, to make sound financial decisions, individuals need to be equipped not only with a basic level of financial knowledge, but also with the skills to apply that knowledge to financial decision making and behaviors.

The federal government plays a wide-ranging role in promoting financial literacy, and the multiagency Financial Literacy and Education Commission, which was created in 2003 by the Fair and Accurate Credit Transactions Act of 2003, was charged with, among other things, developing a national strategy to promote financial literacy and education, coordinating federal efforts, and identifying—and proposing means of eliminating—areas of overlap and duplication.[2] The commission is currently comprised of 21 federal entities; its Chair is the Secretary of the Treasury and its Vice Chair, as established in the Dodd-Frank Wall Street Reform and Consumer Protection Act (Dodd-Frank Act), is the Director of CFPB.[3] A wide variety of other organizations also provide financial literacy resources, including nonprofit community-based organizations; consumer advocacy organizations; financial services companies; trade associations; employers; and local, state, and federal government entities. Some financial literacy initiatives are aimed at the general population, while others target certain audiences, such as low-income individuals, military personnel, high school students, seniors, or homeowners. Similarly, some financial literacy initiatives cover a broad array of concepts and financial topics, while others target specific topics, such as managing credit, investing, purchasing a home, saving for retirement, or avoiding fraudulent or abusive practices.

Efforts to improve financial literacy can take many forms. These can include one-on-one counseling; curricula taught in a classroom setting; workshops or information sessions; print materials, such as brochures

---

[2]Pub. L. No. 108-159, Title V, 117 Stat. 1952, 2003 (2003) (codified at 20 U.S.C. §§ 9701-08).

[3]Pub. L. No. 111-203, Title X, § 1013(d), 124 Stat. 1971, 1956 (2010), 20 U.S.C. § 9702(d).

and pamphlets; and mass media campaigns that can include advertisements in magazines and newspapers or on television, radio, or billboards. Many entities use the Internet to provide financial education, which can include information and training materials, practical tools such as budget worksheets and loan and retirement calculators, and interactive financial games. Youth-focused financial education programs are generally tied to a school curriculum.

Federal Agencies Spent about $68 Million on Financial Literacy Activities in Fiscal Year 2010

In fiscal year 2010, the federal government spent about $68 million on 15 of its 16 significant financial literacy programs and about $137 million on 4 programs providing housing counseling, which can include elements of financial education.

Costs for Financial Literacy Activities

We identified 16 significant financial literacy programs or activities within the federal government in fiscal year 2010.[4] As seen in table 1, the estimated cost for 15 of these programs and activities was $68 million.[5] This figure does not include estimated costs for CFPB, which was created during fiscal year 2010, or costs related to housing counseling, which is discussed separately.

---

[4]The program and cost data included in this report reflect fiscal year 2010 because these data were originally collected as part of our most recent effort to report on duplication, fragmentation, and overlap in federal programs (GAO-12-342SP), which used fiscal year 2010 as its time frame. We have defined "significant" as those financial literacy and education programs or activities that were relatively comprehensive in scope or scale and included financial literacy as a key objective rather than a tangential goal. Additional information about our criteria for significant programs or activities appears later in this report.

[5]This report updates cost information provided in our February 2012 report, GAO-12-342SP, which did not include cost information for the Office of Personnel Management and the Department of Defense. All costs are for fiscal year 2010, with the exception of the Board of Governors of the Federal Reserve System, costs for which are from calendar year 2010.

Table 1: Estimates for Costs of 16 Federal Financial Literacy Activities, Fiscal Year 2010

Agency	Program or activity	FY 2010 estimate for portion of program costs attributed to financial literacy activities	Notes
Board of Governors of the Federal Reserve System	Division of Consumer and Community Affairs and Office of Public Affairs	$1,029,885	Estimate of calendar year 2010 costs provided by agency staff
Consumer Financial Protection Bureau	Office of Financial Education and other offices	Not applicable	Agency had not yet been created at the beginning of FY 2010
Department of Agriculture	Family and Consumer Economics programs	8,433,500	Estimate of FY 2010 costs provided by agency staff
Department of Defense	Personal Financial Management Program (located within Family Support Centers)	38,000,000	Estimate of FY 2010 costs provided by agency staff
Department of Education	Excellence in Economic Education Program	1,447,000	FY 2010 obligations
	Financial Education for College Access and Success Program	1,700,000	FY 2010 obligations
Department of Health and Human Services	National Education and Resource Center on Women and Retirement Planning	245,763	FY 2010 obligations
Department of Labor	Saving Matters Retirement Savings Education Campaign	365,387	Estimate of FY 2010 costs provided by agency staff
	Wi$eUp	170,000	Estimate of FY 2010 costs provided by agency staff
Department of the Treasury	Office of Financial Education and Financial Access (including staff support for the Financial Literacy and Education Commission, and other initiatives)	1,300,000	Estimate of FY 2010 costs provided by agency staff
Federal Deposit Insurance Corporation	Money Smart Financial Education Program	2,749,594	Estimate of FY 2010 costs provided by agency staff
Federal Trade Commission	Division of Consumer and Business Education	784,904	Estimate of FY 2010 costs provided by agency staff
Office of the Comptroller of the Currency	Consumer education activities	450,000	Estimate of FY 2010 costs provided by agency staff.
Office of Personnel Management	Retirement Readiness NOW	200,000	Estimate of FY 2010 costs provided by agency staff
Securities and Exchange Commission	Office of Investor Education and Advocacy	2,000,000	Estimate of FY 2010 costs provided by agency staff
Social Security Administration	Financial Literacy Research Consortium	9,221,000	Estimate of FY 2010 costs provided by agency staff
Total		**$68,097,033**	

Source: GAO analysis based on federal budget documents and cost estimates provided by agency staff.

Two of these federal financial literacy programs or activities were funded through a congressional appropriation for the specified program. The Excellence in Economic Education Program was appropriated about $1.45 million in fiscal year 2010, and the Department of Education obligated almost all of the amount to fund a single 5-year grant to a national nonprofit education organization. The National Education and Resource Center on Women and Retirement Planning was appropriated $249,000 for fiscal year 2010, and the Department of Health and Human Services obligated about $246,000 of that amount that year.

For most of the other programs, financial literacy activities were typically not organized as separate budget line items or cost centers within federal agencies. Instead, financial literacy activities were often one element of a broader effort that itself may or may not have had discrete funding. In these cases, we asked agency staff to estimate the portion of program costs that could be attributed to financial literacy activities. This typically entailed estimating the cost for the portion of staff time devoted to financial literacy, and sometimes also included the cost of contracts, printing, or other resources related to financial literacy activities. Because the methods for estimating costs varied, these costs may not be fully comparable across agencies.

We did not collect comprehensive information for costs subsequent to fiscal year 2010, but spending on many financial literacy programs has been in flux since that time. For example, the Social Security Administration's Financial Literacy Research Consortium and the Financial Education for College Access and Success Program did not receive new funding in fiscal years 2011 or 2012, and the Excellence in Economic Education Program did not receive funding for fiscal year 2012. In addition, at least two agencies—the Department of the Treasury (Treasury) and the Board of Governors of the Federal Reserve System— told us that their staffing resources devoted to financial literacy have declined since 2010. We did not identify any new federal financial literacy programs created since fiscal year 2010 other than CFPB, which was being formed as an agency that year.

Costs for Housing Counseling Activities

As shown in table 2, two federal agencies and a federally chartered nonprofit corporation spent about $136.6 million on housing counseling efforts during fiscal year 2010.[6] We have separated out the costs of housing counseling from other financial literacy activities because financial education typically is only a limited aspect of most housing counseling, which often largely consists of one-on-one assistance to address individual situations.

Table 2: Estimates for Costs of Four Federal Housing Counseling Programs, Fiscal Year 2010

Agency	Program or activity	FY 2010 estimate	Notes
Department of Housing and Urban Development	Housing Counseling Assistance Program	$65,420,000	FY 2010 obligations
Department of the Treasury	Financial Education and Counseling Pilot Program	4,150,000	FY 2010 appropriation
NeighborWorks America	National Foreclosure Mitigation Counseling Program	65,000,000	FY 2010 obligations
	Other housing counseling activities	2,000,000	Estimate of FY 2010 costs provided by agency staff
Total		**$136,570,000**	

Source: GAO analysis based on federal budget documents and cost estimates provided by agency staff.

As seen above, the Department of Housing and Urban Development (HUD) obligated about $65.4 million during fiscal year 2010 for its Housing Counseling Assistance Program, which it used for certifying and overseeing housing counseling providers, training housing counselors, and providing counseling agencies with competitive grants. HUD also has 15 other active programs that have some housing counseling component or allow some portion of their funding to be used for housing counseling.[7] In addition, NeighborWorks America, a federally chartered nonprofit

---

[6]Programs within other agencies, such as the Department of Defense and the Department of Veterans Affairs, also provide some elements of housing counseling.

[7]These programs are the Federal Housing Administration's Home Equity Conversion Mortgage; Community Development Block Grant; HOME Investment Partnerships Program; Second Mortgage Assistance for First-Time Homebuyers; Rural Housing Stability Grant Program; Public Housing Operating Fund; Section 8 Tenant-Based Rental Assistance Homeownership Option; Demolition and Disposition of Public Housing; Family Self-Sufficiency; Public Housing Resident Homeownership Programs; Conversion of Distressed Public Housing to Tenant-Based Assistance; Low Income Housing Preservation and Resident Homeownership Act Prepayment Options; Native American Housing Assistance and Self Determination Act Housing Block Grants; Native Hawaiian Housing Block Grants; and Section 8 Rental Assistance.

corporation, was appropriated $65 million for the National Foreclosure Mitigation Counseling Program during fiscal year 2010, of which it expended $59.4 million in grants for counseling, $3 million for training counselors, and $2.6 million for administrative purposes, according to agency staff. The organization also estimated that it spent about $2 million on other housing counseling activities—primarily prepurchase counseling—from funds it received through a separate congressional appropriation.[8] Treasury's Financial Education and Counseling Pilot Program, created by the Housing and Economic Recovery Act of 2008, provided $4.15 million in grants during fiscal year 2010 to provide counseling to prospective homebuyers.[9] Congress designated $3.15 million for an eligible organization in Hawaii, and Treasury also selected three additional organizations to receive grants.

In general, funding for housing counseling has varied in recent years. For example, HUD received no appropriated funds for its Housing Counseling Assistance Program in fiscal year 2011, but funding was restored to $45 million in fiscal year 2012. The agency has requested $55 million for the program in its fiscal year 2013 budget request, which it said would help support the Office of Housing Counseling, a new office created by the Dodd-Frank Act. The Financial Education and Counseling Pilot Program was appropriated no funds in fiscal years 2011 and 2012.

---

[8]According to NeighborWorks staff, in addition to its direct appropriations from Congress, NeighborWorks also received two grants from HUD related to housing counseling in fiscal year 2010. We have included the funding for those grants in the cost estimate for HUD rather than NeighborWorks. One grant was for $1,250,501 for comprehensive counseling, and the second was for $500,000 for counseling under the Home Equity Conversion Mortgage program, which allows homeowners age 62 or older to tap into the equity in their homes by borrowing against the value of their home.

[9]Pub. L. No. 110-289, § 1132, 122 Stat. 2654, 2727 (2008) (codified at 12 U.S.C. §1701x Note).

Some Federal Financial Literacy Efforts Overlap and May Offer Opportunities for Consolidation

Financial Literacy Efforts Are Spread across Multiple Federal Agencies

Federal financial literacy efforts are carried out by multiple federal programs and agencies. As shown in table 3, in fiscal year 2010 there were 16 significant federal financial literacy programs or activities among 14 federal agencies, as well as 4 housing counseling programs among 2 federal agencies and a federally chartered nonprofit corporation. These programs and activities covered a wide range of topics and target audiences and used a variety of delivery mechanisms.

Table 3: Description and Target Audience for Significant Federal Financial Literacy and Housing Counseling Programs and Activities, Fiscal Year 2010

Financial Literacy			
Agency	Program or activity	Description	Target audience
Board of Governors of the Federal Reserve System	Division of Consumer and Community Affairs and Office of Public Affairs	Up-to-date web resources on regulatory changes regarding financial products and services, calculators, and information and tools on terms and disclosures for credit card accounts, overdraft protection programs, gift cards and credit scores. Website offers resources for teachers and students of various ages and knowledge levels via educational games, classroom lesson plans, online publications, and multimedia tools.	Adult consumers and students
Consumer Financial Protection Bureau	Office of Financial Education and other offices	The Office of Financial Education, Office of Servicemember Affairs, Office of Fair Lending and Equal Opportunity, and Office of Financial Protection for Older Americans plan to develop and implement initiatives to educate and empower consumers in general and specific target groups to make informed financial decisions.	Consumers, servicemembers and their families, individuals who are 62 years or older
Department of Agriculture	Family and Consumer Economics programs	The National Institute of Food and Agriculture provides funding to land-grant colleges and universities and to state and county extension offices to support research and education, including outreach events related to personal financial topics.	Youth, rural families, elderly, other financially vulnerable populations

Department of Defense	Personal Financial Management Program (located within Family Support Centers)	Personal financial managers on military installations provide financial education programs and counseling services designed to help servicemembers reach their financial goals. Services range from consultation on financial management, budgeting, and saving, to debt reduction strategies, consumer advocacy and complaint resolution, financial workshops, retirement planning, housing issues and referrals, and education programs for youth and teens.	Servicemembers and their families
Department of Education	Excellence in Economic Education Program	Competitive grant awarded to an organization that conducts activities, and makes subgrants to other organizations, to improve the quality of student understanding of personal finance and economics.	Students in kindergarten through grade 12
	Financial Education for College Access and Success Program	Supports state-led efforts to develop, implement, and evaluate personal finance instructional materials and teacher training intended to aid students in making financial aid decisions in relation to postsecondary education.	Students in middle and high-school—generally grades 6-12
Department of Health and Human Services	National Education and Resource Center on Women and Retirement Planning	Provides women access to a one-stop gateway on retirement, care giving, health, and planning for long-term care.	Low-income women, women of color, women with limited English proficiency
Department of Labor	Saving Matters Retirement Savings Education Campaign	Workplace campaign to promote retirement savings and understanding of federal retirement law using interactive web tools, print publications, website, public service announcements, seminars, workshops, videos, and webcasts.	Employees, employers, small businesses
	Wi$eUp	Eight-module financial education curriculum targeting women that covers topics that include money basics, credit, saving and investing, insurance, retirement planning, and financial security. Offered online or in a classroom setting.	Generation X and Y women
Department of the Treasury	Office of Financial Education and Financial Access	A variety of financial literacy activities, including Money Math (four-lesson curriculum integrating personal finance and math topics), the National Financial Capability Challenge (provides teaching resources and encouragement and tests high school students on personal finance topics), Bank On USA (program encouraging access to mainstream financial institutions), MyMoney.gov (website on federal financial literacy resources), and staff support for the Financial Literacy and Education Commission.	All populations
Federal Deposit Insurance Corporation	Money Smart Financial Education Program	Eleven-module financial education curriculum for adults designed to enhance basic financial skills and create positive banking relationships, available in nine languages. Eight-module version is available for young adults. The curriculum is available in instructor-led, computer-based instruction, and podcast (Mp3) formats.	Low- to moderate-income adults outside the financial mainstream and youth ages 12-20

Federal Trade Commission	Division of Consumer and Business Education	Multi-media resources covering topics such as credit, credit repair, debt collection, job hunting, job scams, managing mortgage payments, avoiding foreclosure rescue scams, and identity theft.	Consumers
Office of the Comptroller of the Currency	Consumer education activities	Websites, consumer advisories, public service announcements, community outreach, and print and radio advertisements aimed at educating consumers about banking and other financial issues.	Consumers
Office of Personnel Management	Retirement Readiness NOW	Retirement education strategy designed to provide information that will help federal employees plan for retirement and calculate the investment needed to meet retirement goals.	Federal employees
Securities and Exchange Commission	Office of Investor Education and Advocacy	Provides information to help individual investors evaluate current and potential investments, make informed decisions, and avoid fraud.	Investors
Social Security Administration	Financial Literacy Research Consortium	Supported 2-year cooperative agreements with Boston College, RAND Corporation, and the University of Wisconsin to develop innovative materials and programs to help Americans plan for a secure retirement.	Adults preparing for retirement
Housing Counseling and Foreclosure Mitigation			
Department of Housing and Urban Development	Housing Counseling Assistance Program	Certifies and oversees housing counseling providers. Provides competitive grants to approved housing counseling agencies that provide prepurchase and postpurchase counseling, assistance to renters, homeless populations, and those seeking to resolve mortgage delinquency. Counseling may take place in person, over the phone, or via a self-study computer module or workbook.	Low-to moderate-income families
Department of the Treasury	Financial Education and Counseling Pilot Program	Competitive grants to organizations to provide financial education and counseling to prospective homebuyers.	Prospective homebuyers
NeighborWorks America	National Foreclosure Mitigation Counseling Program	Competitive grants to housing counseling agencies to provide one-on-one counseling services for foreclosure prevention.	Homeowners at risk of foreclosure
	Other housing counseling activities	Expendable grants for which housing counseling is an eligible activity.	Current and prospective homeowners

Source: GAO analysis based on information from federal agencies and interviews with agency staff.

In prior work, we cited a 2009 report that had identified 56 federal financial literacy programs among 20 agencies.[10] That report, issued by the RAND Corporation, was based on a survey conducted by Treasury and the Department of Education that had asked federal agencies to self-identify their financial literacy efforts. However, our subsequent analysis of these 56 programs found a high degree of inconsistency in how different agencies defined financial literacy programs or efforts and whether they counted related efforts as one or multiple programs. We believe that our count of 16 significant federal financial literacy programs or activities and 4 housing counseling programs is based on a more consistent set of criteria.[11] (See app. II for a crosswalk between the 56 programs cited in a previous report and the 20 programs highlighted in this report.) We defined "significant" financial literacy programs or activities as those that were relatively comprehensive in scope or scale—that is, financial literacy was a key element rather than a minimal component or tangential goal. We did not include programs or activities that (1) provided financial information related to the administration of the program itself—such as information on applying for student financial aid or evaluating Medicare choices—rather than information aimed at increasing the beneficiaries' financial literacy and comprehension more generally; (2) were purely internal to the agency, such as information provided to agency employees on their employment and retirement benefits; or (3) represented individualized services or advice, such as assistance with tax preparation.[12] Apart from the programs cited in the tables above, some additional federal agencies address financial literacy on a smaller scale. For example, the website of the Federal Deposit Insurance Corporation (FDIC) includes such things as tips on banking and protecting your money, and information on foreclosure prevention,

---

[10]GAO, *List of Selected Federal Programs That Have Similar or Overlapping Objectives, Provide Similar Services, or Are Fragmented Across Government Missions*, GAO-11-474R (Washington, D. C.: Mar. 18, 2011); and GAO-11-318SP. Angela A. Hung, Kata Mihaly, and Joanne K. Yoong (RAND Corporation), "Federal Financial and Economic Literacy Education Programs, 2009" (Santa Monica, Calif.: 2010). http://www.rand.org/content/dam/rand/pubs/technical_reports/2010/RAND_TR857.pdf.

[11]Our review was based on programs in place in fiscal year 2010; as noted earlier, at least three of the programs in place at that time were not funded in fiscal year 2012.

[12]Although the financial literacy activities of the Department of Defense's Family Support Centers are largely internal to the agency, we made an exception and included them because they serve more than 7 million individuals and provide a broad range of counseling and services.

identity theft, and deposit insurance. In addition, the website of the Commodity Futures Trading Commission provides information on fraud awareness and prevention related to trading futures and options.

Fragmentation of financial literacy programs has evolved over a number of years, as a result both of statutory requirements and efforts undertaken at the initiative of federal agencies in addressing their missions.[13] Congress directed the creation of some programs and initiatives, examples of which include the following:

- The Office of Personnel Management's Retirement Readiness NOW program and the development of a retirement financial literacy strategy for federal employees were required by the Thrift Savings Plan Open Elections Act of 2004.[14]

- The Financial Education and Counseling Pilot Program was created by the Housing and Economic Recovery Act of 2008.[15]

- The Financial Education for College Access and Success Program was authorized under the Fund for the Improvement of Education Program under the Elementary and Secondary Education Act of 1965.[16]

- The National Foreclosure Mitigation Counseling Program was authorized through the Consolidated Appropriations Act, 2008, which sought to address the mortgage foreclosure crisis by providing homeowner counseling and strengthening the nation's counseling capacity.[17]

---

[13]We define fragmentation to refer to those circumstances in which more than one federal agency (or more than one organization within an agency) is involved in the same broad area of national need.

[14]Pub. L. 108-469, § 2, 118 Stat. 3892 (2004), 5 U.S.C. § 8350 Note.

[15]Pub. L. No. 110-289, § 1132, 122 Stat. 2654, 2727 (2008), 12 U.S.C. § 1701x Note.

[16]Elementary and Secondary Education Act of 1965, as amended, Pub. L. No. 89-10, 79 Stat. 27, 20 U.S.C. §§ 7243-7243b.

[17]Pub. L No. 110-161, Div. K, Title III, 121 Stat. 1844, 2441 (2008).

- CFPB was created by the Dodd-Frank Act, which specified the creation of the bureau's Office of Financial Education and its role in promoting financial literacy.[18]

Other financial literacy programs were initiated by agencies as part of their mission. For example, in line with the Securities and Exchange Commission's (SEC) mission as the primary overseer and regulator of the U.S. securities markets, the agency created the Office of Investor Education and Advocacy, which gives investors information to evaluate current and potential investments, make informed decisions, and avoid fraudulent schemes. Similarly, the Federal Trade Commission's (FTC) financial literacy efforts have stemmed from its responsibilities for enforcing laws and regulations against unfair or deceptive acts or practices and protecting consumers in the marketplace.

Having multiple federal agencies involved in financial literacy efforts can have certain advantages. Some agencies have deep and long-standing expertise and experience addressing a specific issue area. For example, HUD has long been a repository for information on housing issues, SEC on investment issues, and the Department of Labor and Social Security Administration on retirement issues. Some agencies also have deep knowledge and ties to particular populations and may be the most efficient and natural conduit to providing them with information and services, as with the Department of Defense's (DOD) role in providing financial information and counseling to servicemembers and their families. In addition, providing information from multiple sources or in multiple formats can increase consumer access and the likelihood of educating more people. We have previously reported that different populations respond to different types of delivery mechanisms, such as one-on-one credit counseling, employer-provided retirement seminars, and classroom-based education.[19]

At the same time, fragmentation increases the risk of inefficiency and duplication of efforts. Our detailed review of financial literacy efforts across the federal government has uncovered no duplication—that is, cases where two or more agencies or programs were engaging in the

---

[18]Dodd-Frank Act, § 1011, 124 Stat. 1376, 1964 (2010), 12 U.S.C. § 5491.

[19]GAO, *Financial Literacy: A Federal Certification Process for Providers Would Pose Challenges*, GAO-11-614 (Washington, D.C.: June 28, 2011).

same efforts and providing the same services to the same beneficiaries. In our analysis of the 20 significant financial literacy and housing counseling programs, we found that programs and efforts had differing focuses in terms of subject matter, target audience, or delivery method. This finding is largely consistent with prior reviews of the federal government's financial literacy efforts. In 2006, the Financial Literacy and Education Commission reported that it had studied federal financial literacy programs or resources and said it found minimal overlap and duplication among programs, noting that even when different agencies' programs sometimes appeared similar, closer inspection revealed important differences in things like the target audience, delivery platform, or specific content. In response to a recommendation we made that the commission engage an independent third party to assess these issues, two subsequent studies were conducted. The first study, contracted by Treasury to assess federal programs, reported little evidence of duplication of programs or resources based on comparisons of the intended program goals and targeted audiences of the assessed programs and major resources.[20] The second study resulted in the previously discussed 2009 report by the RAND Corporation, which sought to create a comprehensive catalog of existing federal financial literacy programs. It did not identify clear duplication, but it did note that multiple areas of overlap in subject matter and target audiences warranted more thorough investigation.

Our review did identify cases of overlap—that is, multiple agencies or programs with similar goals and activities. For example, as shown earlier, in fiscal year 2010 there were four discrete housing counseling programs or activities, which were administered by HUD, NeighborWorks America, and Treasury.[21] HUD's Housing Counseling Assistance Program funded a wide range of housing counseling, including prepurchase and postpurchase counseling and counseling related to foreclosure mitigation and prevention of predatory lending, as well as counseling services for

---

[20]Sarah Baughman, *Financial Literacy and Education Commission Independent Evaluation Final Report* (Blacksburg, Va.: May 25, 2009).

[21]Programs at DOD and the Department of Veterans Affairs also provide some elements of housing counseling. DOD's Military OneSource and Military and Family Life Consultant Program provide foreclosure counseling for servicemembers returning home from active duty abroad, and the Department of Veterans Affairs has loan counselors that address housing issues in its Regional Loan Centers to help veterans facing foreclosure or other financial problems.

renters and homeless populations.[22] Treasury's Financial Education and Counseling Pilot Program had goals similar to HUD's program, although it focused solely on prepurchase counseling and was intended, in part, to establish innovative program models for organizations to carry out effective counseling services. NeighborWorks also provided some prepurchase counseling and administered the foreclosure mitigation counseling program designed to help homeowners work with lenders to cure delinquencies. HUD and NeighborWorks meet regularly and closely coordinate activities to be complementary, according to HUD staff.

Similarly, five different financial literacy programs were directed at youth or young adults in fiscal year 2010. Three of these programs—Money Smart for Young Adults, Money Math, and the National Financial Capability Challenge—delivered information on similar topics, such as saving, budgeting, and borrowing, largely via instructor-led lesson plans. The Excellence in Economic Education Program and the Financial Education for College Access and Success Program both supported the development of personal finance instructional materials and teacher training on personal finance. In addition, FTC addresses youth financial literacy through an interactive website where youth can play games, design advertisements, and learn about activities related to target marketing, supply and demand, privacy protection, and bogus offers. The website of the Board of Governors of the Federal Reserve System also offers interactive games and classroom activities on its website for youth and young adults. Treasury staff told us that while all of these programs serve youth or young adults, there are significant variations among them in approach and in content. The staff noted, for example, that the goal of the National Financial Capability Challenge is to encourage the teaching of financial topics, rather than to provide content, and that the curricula of the Money Math and Money Smart for Young Adults programs differ substantially from each other.

Another example of overlap can be found in two federal financial literacy programs designed specifically for adult women. The Department of Labor's Wi$eUp program targeted Generation X and Y women—women generally born between the mid-1960s and the mid-1990s—and the

---

[22]Prepurchase counseling generally helps potential homebuyers learn about buying a home and explains the financial responsibilities of homeownership. Postpurchase counseling includes topics such as foreclosure mitigation, budgeting, and home maintenance.

Department of Health and Human Services' National Education and Resource Center on Women and Retirement Planning targeted traditionally hard-to-reach women, such as low-income women, women of color, and women with limited English proficiency. Both programs cover some of the same topic areas, such as retirement planning, investing, and money basics such as budgeting, saving, and banking. However, staff at the Department of Labor and the Department of Health and Human Services noted that the programs target different users, have different goals, and engage in different activities—for example, Wi$eUp is an online and classroom curriculum, while the National Resource Center uses peer counselors and offers information through model programs, workshops tailored to meet special needs, and print and web-based publications.

Creation of CFPB May Provide Opportunities for Consolidation

Additional overlap is evident with the activities of CFPB, which was created by the Dodd-Frank Act and became a standing organization in July 2011. The act established within CFPB an Office of Financial Education and charged it with developing and implementing initiatives intended to educate and empower consumers to make better informed financial decisions. Specifically, the office was directed to provide opportunities for consumers to access, among other things, financial counseling; information to assist consumers with understanding credit products, histories, and scores; information about savings and borrowing tools; and assistance in developing long-term savings strategies and wealth building. The duties of this office are in some ways similar to those of Treasury's Office of Financial Access, Financial Education, and Consumer Protection, a small office that also seeks to broadly improve Americans' financial literacy.[23] Treasury established this office in 2002 and tasked it with developing and implementing financial education policy initiatives and overseeing and coordinating Treasury's outreach efforts. Further, the Dodd-Frank Act charged CFPB with developing and implementing a strategy on improving the financial literacy of consumers, even though the Financial Literacy and Education Commission already has its own statutory mandate to develop, and update as necessary, a national strategy for financial literacy. CFPB staff told us that its own national strategy for financial literacy will serve as an operating plan that

---

[23]In April 2012, Treasury changed the name of the Office of Financial Education and Financial Access to the Office of Financial Access, Financial Education, and Consumer Protection, and the office has taken on new functions related to consumer protection.

is distinct from, but broadly aligned with, the commission's national strategy. Staff involved in financial literacy from Treasury and CFPB told us that they meet regularly and that the two agencies are working closely together to ensure collaboration and avoid duplication.

CFPB also has other offices that are charged with financial literacy duties that are in some ways similar to those of other federal agencies. For example, the Dodd-Frank Act created within CFPB an Office of Servicemember Affairs, which is responsible for, among other things, developing and implementing initiatives intended to educate servicemembers and their families and empower them to make better informed decisions regarding consumer financial products and services, monitoring complaints, and coordinating efforts among federal and state agencies regarding consumer protection measures. These activities potentially overlap with those of DOD, whose Personal Financial Managers on military installations provide financial educational programs, partnerships, counseling, legal protections, and other resources designed to help servicemembers and their families. Staff of CFPB's Office of Servicemember Affairs told us that the office has been actively reaching out to servicemembers where they live in order to assess their needs, and between January 2011 and May 2012, the office held 84 events attended by more than 24,000 people and visited 37 military installations and National Guard units. Staff also told us that they have taken several steps to avoid duplicating DOD's Financial Readiness Program. For example, they said they will be focusing on reaching servicemembers in the Delayed Entry Program, a period prior to boot camp during which DOD does not yet engage in financial education. In addition, CFPB staff said they have been meeting monthly with DOD's Deputy Assistant Secretary of Defense for Military Community and Family Policy and his staff to coordinate their activities to avoid duplication across agencies. CFPB and DOD have also developed two Joint Statements of Principles, one on how they are going to handle complaints and the other on educational efforts and small-dollar lending.

In addition, CFPB and several other agencies provide financial literacy services that target older Americans. The Dodd-Frank Act created the Office of Financial Protection for Older Americans within CFPB and charged the office to develop goals for programs that provide financial literacy and counseling to help seniors recognize the warning signs of unfair, deceptive, or abusive practices, and protect themselves from such practices. These activities potentially overlap with those of FTC, which also plays a role in helping seniors avoid unfair and deceptive practices. For example, FTC has provided information to seniors on a range of topics, such as obtaining credit over the age of 62, avoiding charity fraud, recognizing and reporting telemarketing fraud, and avoiding scammers who may pose as friends, family, or government agencies. In an effort to work together and avoid duplication, CFPB and FTC finalized a memorandum of understanding in January 2012 to help, among other things, cooperate on consumer education efforts, promote consistency of messages, and maximize the use of educational resources. The Dodd-Frank Act also charged the Office of Financial Protection for Older Americans to develop goals for programs that provide one-on-one financial counseling on long-term savings and later-life economic security. As discussed earlier, the Department of Labor's Saving Matters Retirement Savings Education Campaign also plays a role in educating consumers on retirement issues and the Social Security Administration had a special initiative, as part of an earlier strategic plan, to encourage saving and to inform the public about its programs. In January 2012, staff at CFPB told us that the Office of Financial Protection for Older Americans had only recently become fully staffed and that the office had begun working with other federal and state agencies to identify best practices for educating and counseling senior citizens, identifying unfair and deceptive practices targeting this population, and advocating on their behalf.

Other potential areas of overlap include CFPB's Office of Fair Lending and Equal Opportunity, which plays a role in providing education on fair lending, as do the Office of the Comptroller of the Currency, FDIC, and FTC. CFPB has also created an Office for Students to work with complaints and questions regarding student loans. However, the Department of Education already has a number of web-based tools in place to help students understand financial aid and student loans. CFPB staff told us that one key distinction is that CFPB addresses private student loans, while the Department of Education addresses federally supported student loans. They also noted that they are coordinating with the Department of Education and have developed a memorandum of understanding with the department, and have jointly designed a standard student loan award letter and fact sheet.

The Dodd-Frank Act gave CFPB a primary role in addressing financial literacy, and the agency's Office of Financial Education—staffed at 10 full-time equivalents as of June 2012—has significant financial literacy resources relative to many other agencies. Yet there are similarities in mission between CFPB's statutory responsibilities and those of certain other federal entities. As we have noted in the past, federal programs contributing to the same or similar results should collaborate to help ensure that goals are consistent and, as appropriate, program efforts are mutually reinforcing.[24] Collaborating agencies should work together to define and agree on their respective roles and responsibilities and, in doing so, clarify who will do what and organize their joint and individual efforts. As noted above, during its initial development, CFPB has been meeting with other federal entities to coordinate their efforts. Ensuring clear delineation of the respective roles and responsibilities between CFPB and agencies with overlapping financial literacy responsibilities is essential to help ensure efficient use of resources.

The creation of multiple efforts within the federal government to address financial literacy has been the result of both legislation and initiatives within agencies. We have noted in the past that fragmentation in government programs often is the result of an adaptive and responsive federal government.[25] As new needs were identified, the common response has been a proliferation of responsibilities and roles to federal departments and agencies, perhaps targeted to a new audience or involving a new subject area. However, overlap and fragmentation among government programs or activities can, in some circumstances, lead to inefficiency, and the President and some members of Congress have set a goal of reorganizing and consolidating federal agencies to reduce the number of overlapping government programs.[26] In addition, as noted earlier, the multiagency Financial Literacy and Education Commission was charged by statute with proposing means of eliminating overlap and duplication among federal financial literacy activities.[27] The creation of CFPB, which will play a primary role in financial literacy, provides an opportunity for the commission and its member agencies to consider options for consolidating federal financial literacy efforts, which could help ensure the most efficient and effective use of federal resources in this area. While our February 2012 report stated that we expected to suggest

---

[24]GAO, *Results-Oriented Government: Practices That Can Help Enhance and Sustain Collaboration among Federal Agencies*, GAO-06-15 (Washington, D.C.: Oct. 21, 2005).

[25]GAO, *Managing for Results: Using the Results Act to Address Mission Fragmentation and Program Overlap*, GAO/AIMD-97-146 (Washington, D.C.: Aug. 29, 1997).

[26]For example, see Executive Office of the President, *Building a 21st Century Government by Cutting Duplication, Fragmentation, and Waste* (Washington, D.C.: Feb. 28, 2012).

[27]Pub. L. No. 108-159, § 514(f)(2)(d), 117 Stat. 1952, 2006 (Dec. 4, 2003) (codified at 20 U.S.C. § 9703(f)(2)(d)).

that Congress consider options for such consolidation, the commission is better positioned to do so and this would be consistent with its statutory responsibility to address overlap and duplication.

Agencies Coordinate Their Efforts, but Opportunities Exist to Better Address the Appropriate Allocation of Resources

In addition to CFPB's efforts cited above, there has been a significant amount of coordination among other federal agencies with regard to their financial literacy efforts, as well as evidence of collaboration among federal agencies and state, local, nonprofit, and private entities. The Financial Literacy and Education Commission has played a key role in fostering this coordination and collaboration. However, its national strategy does not include a discussion of the appropriate allocation of federal resources.

Coordination and Collaboration Occur through a Variety of Means

Federal agencies involved in addressing financial literacy have a variety of mechanisms for coordinating their efforts, examples of which include the following:

- The Government Interagency Group is a working group of program-level staff from federal agencies that address financial literacy. The group meets three times a year to share ideas and best practices. The group is organized by the American Savings Education Council, a nonprofit organization and national coalition of public and private sector institutions focused on savings and retirement planning.

- The Department of Education, FDIC, and the National Credit Union Administration signed an agreement in November 2010 designed to encourage partnerships between schools, financial institutions, federal grantees, and other stakeholders to educate students about saving, budgeting and making wise financial decisions.

- SEC has partnered with the Department of Labor to develop guidance to help individuals understand the operations and risks of target-date fund investments, which are often mutual funds that change automatically to become more conservative as the fund's target date approaches. SEC has also worked with the Internal Revenue Service to include an insert about SEC's investor education resources, including its Investor.gov education website, in the mailing of tax refund checks.

- As part of its Retirement Financial Literacy and Education Strategy for federal employees, the Office of Personnel Management has efforts under way to provide training and tools to the benefits officers of individual federal agencies, and to identify existing resources that federal agencies might use for the financial education of their employees.

- The Department of Labor and the Social Security Administration have worked together with AARP—a nonprofit organization focused on people age 50 and over—to host workshops for workers nearing retirement.

In addition to interagency coordination, the federal government has certain mechanisms in place to coordinate or partner with nonfederal entities, including states and localities and nonprofit and private entities. In January 2010, the President's Advisory Council on Financial Capability was created by executive order.[28] The council was tasked with a number of specific charges, including advising the President and the Secretary of the Treasury on: financial education efforts, promoting financial products and services that are beneficial to consumers (especially low- and moderate-income consumers), and promoting understanding of effective use of such products and services. In its January 2012 interim report, the council recommended that Treasury support a newly created private-sector award program recognizing employers that provide outstanding financial education to their employees.[29] The council meets regularly and has established subcommittees to address issues related to research and evaluation, partnerships between the public and private sectors, expanding financial access to low- and moderate-income households, and youth.

---

[28]Exec. Order No. 13,530, 75 Fed. Reg. 5481 (Jan. 29, 2010). Prior to the President's Advisory Council on Financial Capability, created by President Obama, there was the President's Advisory Council on Financial Literacy, which was created by executive order by President Bush in January 2008. Exec. Order No. 13,455, 73 Fed. Reg. 4445 (Jan. 22, 2008).

[29]U.S. Department of the Treasury, *Interim Report: President's Advisory Council on Financial Capability* (Washington D.C.: Jan. 18, 2012).

To facilitate and advance financial literacy at the state and local levels, the Financial Literacy and Education Commission created the National Financial Education Network for State and Local Governments in April 2007. Network members include state and local agencies and national organizations that share information through activities including periodic conference calls and a web-based database of financial literacy projects and programs.

Some federal agencies also partner with nonprofit and private organizations to expand outreach. Many federal agencies are members of Jump$tart Coalition for Personal Financial Literacy, a nonprofit partnership that focuses on financial literacy for young adults. Treasury partnered with Jump$tart, the University of Missouri-St. Louis and Citigroup to develop Money Math: Lessons for Life, a financial literacy curriculum supplement for educators. FDIC has signed collaboration agreements or reached informal agreements with more than 1,200 active "alliance members" that promote or enhance the implementation of its Money Smart curriculum. Alliance members include financial institutions, schools or other educational service providers, military installations, community-based organizations, faith-based groups, employment and training service providers, government agencies, and other organizations. Likewise, the Board of Governors of the Federal Reserve System participates in Bank On USA programs, which are locally led coalitions of government agencies, financial institutions, and community organizations that focus on financial education and access for individuals and families who do not use mainstream financial institutions.

Federal agencies also collaborate with nonfederal entities with regard to financial literacy through the process of administering grants. For example, HUD provides training, guidance, and technical assistance to a network of community-based counseling agencies that it funds through its Housing Counseling Assistance Program. HUD also works with NeighborWorks, which is partially funded through HUD, in implementing the National Foreclosure Mitigation Counseling Program. Additionally, the Department of Agriculture collaborates with land-grant universities on financial literacy projects through grants provided by its National Institute of Food and Agriculture.[30] Also, DOD has collaborated with land-grant

---

[30]A land-grant college or university is an institution of higher education designated by its state to receive certain federal benefits where the focus is to be on the teaching of agriculture, science, and engineering.

universities to offer programs and classes for military families and veterans.

Federal agencies have also collaborated with academic researchers and organizations on financial literacy research and product development. For example, in October 2008, Treasury and the Department of Agriculture convened a National Research Symposium on Financial Literacy and Education that sought to identify gaps in existing research and develop research priorities. Twenty-nine experts in the fields of behavioral and consumer economics, financial risk assessment, and financial education evaluation joined to summarize existing financial research findings, identify gaps in the literature, and define and prioritize questions for future analysis. In addition, through the Financial Literacy Research Consortium funded in fiscal years 2009 and 2010, the Social Security Administration worked with Boston College, RAND Corporation, and the University of Wisconsin to develop financial literacy educational tools and programs focusing on retirement savings and planning.

The Financial Literacy and Education Commission Has Improved Coordination but Has Not Addressed Resource Allocation

In general, we found that coordination and collaboration among federal agencies with regard to financial literacy has improved in recent years, in large part due to the efforts of the Financial Literacy and Education Commission. As noted earlier, the commission is currently comprised of 21 federal entities and was charged with, among other things, coordinating federal financial literacy efforts and promoting partnerships among federal, state, and local governments; nonprofit organizations; and private enterprises. Before the formation of the commission, agencies had no formal mechanism within the federal government through which to coordinate on financial literacy activities. In a 2006 report, we noted that the commission enhanced communication and collaboration among agencies involved in financial literacy by creating a single focal point for federal agencies to come together on the issue of financial literacy. The commission also developed a national strategy that included calls to action on interagency efforts.[31] Additional activities undertaken by the commission to foster coordination or collaboration include the following:

---

[31]GAO, *Financial Literacy and Education Commission: Further Progress Needed to Ensure an Effective National Strategy*, GAO-07-100 (Washington, D.C.: Dec. 4, 2006).

- *Meetings and working groups.* The commission holds formal meetings three times per year and, at the staff level, has several working groups, each represented by several federal agencies, including teams devoted to implementing the national strategy, promoting research and evaluation, and improving financial access.

- *MyMoney.gov website.* The commission was charged by statute with developing a financial education website that provides a coordinated point of entry for information about federal financial literacy programs and grants. The commission launched the MyMoney.gov website in October 2004.

- *Clearinghouse of research and resources.* The commission is in the process of developing a clearinghouse of federal research and resources on financial literacy. This clearinghouse will aggregate financial literacy research and information across federal agencies in one public website.

- *Reviews of federal activities.* As discussed earlier, the commission and Treasury contracted for two reports that cataloged and reviewed financial literacy efforts across the federal government, which helped inform federal agencies of each other's activities and foster opportunities for coordination and collaboration.

In April 2006, the Financial Literacy and Education Commission issued a national strategy, which it was required by law to develop and modify as necessary, and in December 2010, it issued *Promoting Financial Success in the United States: National Strategy for Financial Literacy 2011.*[32] In our 2006 report, we found that the commission's first national strategy was a useful first step in focusing attention on financial literacy but was largely descriptive rather than strategic. We noted that the strategy only partially included certain characteristics that we consider to be desirable in any national strategy, including a description of resources required to implement the strategy. Our review of the 2011 national strategy indicates that it still does not fully address this element. An effective national

---

[32]Pub. L. No. 108-159, § 514(h), 117 Stat. 1952, 2004 (Dec. 4, 2003) (codified at 20 U.S.C. § 9703(h)). Financial Literacy and Education Commission, *Taking Ownership of the Future: The National Strategy for Financial Literacy* (Washington, D.C.: April 2006), and Financial Literacy and Education Commission, *Promoting Financial Success in the United States: National Strategy for Financial Literacy 2011* (Washington, D.C.: December 2010).

strategy should include a discussion of resources, describing what a strategy will cost, the sources and types of resources needed, and where those resources should be targeted. The 2011 national strategy discusses the consumer education resources that the federal government makes available to consumers, and it sets building public awareness of these resources as a goal. However, the 2011 strategy still does not address the level and type of resources needed to implement the strategy, nor does it review the budgetary resources available to federal agencies for financial literacy efforts and how they might best be allocated. We have noted in the past that the governance structure of the commission presents challenges in addressing resource issues: it relies on the consensus of more than 20 federal agencies, has no independent budget, and has no legal authority to compel member agencies to take any action.[33] However, the commission does have the ability to at least identify resource needs and make recommendations or provide guidance on how Congress or federal agencies might allocate scarce federal financial literacy resources for maximum benefit. Without a clear description of resource needs, policymakers lack information to help direct the strategy's implementation, and without recommendations on resource allocations, policymakers lack information to help ensure the most efficient and effective use of federal funds. Additionally, addressing resource needs and allocations in the commission's national strategy would facilitate its statutory responsibility, discussed earlier, to propose means of eliminating overlap and duplication among federal financial literacy activities.

---

[33]GAO, *Financial Literacy and Education Commission: Progress Made in Fostering Partnerships, but National Strategy Remains Largely Descriptive Rather Than Strategic,* GAO-09-638T (Washington, D.C.: Apr.29, 2009).

Overall Effectiveness of Federal Financial Literacy Programs Is Difficult to Measure, but Additional Evaluation Efforts Are Under Way

Most federal financial literacy activities include an evaluation component, but variation in the types of activities and the methods of evaluation create challenges in comparing results across programs. As we reported in June 2011, relatively few evidence-based evaluations of financial literacy programs have been conducted, limiting what is known about which specific methods and strategies—and which federal financial literacy activities—are most effective.[34] Several federal agencies have efforts under way seeking to determine the most effective approaches and programs.

Agencies Assess Their Financial Literacy Efforts in Various Ways

The wide range of federal financial literacy programs and activities and their evaluation metrics and methods, makes it difficult to systematically assess overall effectiveness or compare results across programs. Among the 20 significant federal financial literacy and housing counseling programs that we reviewed, we found that nearly all had assessed or measured their activities in some manner and, where feasible, many had undertaken some method of seeking to measure outcomes. Some of these evaluations sought to assess the effect of the program on the actual behavior of program participants and some assessed the effect of the program on knowledge, attitudes, or anticipated behavior. As we have reported in the past, in general the ultimate goal of financial education is to favorably affect consumer behavior, such as to promote improved saving and spending habits and wise use of credit. As such, financial literacy program evaluations are most reliable and effective when they measure the programs' impact on consumers' behavior. While there is fairly extensive literature on financial literacy in general, relatively few evaluations of financial literacy programs have been published that use empirical evidence to measure a program's impact on the participants' behavior.[35]

In addition, there are many significant challenges to rigorous and definitive evaluations of financial literacy programs. Outcome-based evaluation can be expensive and methodologically challenging, particularly long-term evaluation using a controlled experimental

---

[34]GAO, *Financial Literacy: A Federal Certification Process for Providers Would Pose Challenges*, GAO-11-614 (Washington, D.C.: June 28, 2011).

[35]GAO-11-614.

methodology, which can be especially time and labor intensive.[36] As well, measuring a change in participant behavior is much more difficult than measuring a gain in knowledge, which can often be captured through a simple exam at program completion. Some financial literacy programs and activities, such as those using broadcast media to disseminate information, may also simply not be well-suited to outcome-based evaluation because the program has no direct contact with the intended audience. Further, given the many variables that can affect consumer behavior and decision making, ascribing long-term changes to a particular program is difficult. In addition, some program activities, such as posting a webpage, may be too small in scope to warrant conducting an outcome evaluation study, so tracking output measures—such as the number of individuals served or the volume of materials distributed—may be the only feasible option. One academic review of financial literacy evaluations found that the majority of financial literacy programs it reviewed measured only program outputs.[37]

Among the federal financial literacy programs and activities we reviewed, we identified a number of cases in which evaluation included at least some assessment of the effect on consumer behavior of activities operated or funded by federal agencies:

- *National Foreclosure Mitigation Counseling Program.* NeighborWorks contracted with the Urban Institute for a study resulting in a series of reports, the most recent of which was published in December 2011, which evaluated program outcomes of the federally funded National Foreclosure Mitigation Counseling program. The study found that among homeowners who received loan modifications, those who received counseling under the program were more likely to avoid entering foreclosure, successfully cure existing foreclosures, or obtain

---

[36]A controlled experimental methodology is a research design that randomly assigns participants to treatment and control groups in order to rigorously analyze the effects of the studied activity.

[37]Angela C. Lyons, Lance Palmer, Koralalage S. U. Jayaratne, and Erik Scherpf, "Are We Making the Grade? A National Overview of Financial Education and Program Evaluation," *The Journal of Consumer Affairs* 40 (2006): 208-35.

favorable loan modifications than those who did not receive the counseling.[38]

- *U.S. Army personal financial management training.* In 2009, staff at the Board of Governors of the Federal Reserve System conducted a study of a U.S. Army personal financial management training, which included a 2-day financial education course taught by college staff for young servicemembers enlisted at a Texas army base. Participants were surveyed on their financial behaviors 6 months after completing the course and compared with a control group of soldiers who did not take the course. After controlling for other factors, the study found that the financial education course did not have a significant effect on most of the soldiers' financial behaviors, such as comparison shopping, saving, and paying bills on time.[39]

- *Money Smart.* FDIC collaborated in an independent evaluation of the Money Smart program in 2003 that measured its effectiveness on a sample of adult program participants who did not have accounts at banks or other mainstream financial institutions. The study found that 80 percent of those who completed Money Smart said they intended to open a bank account, although it did not collect data on whether they actually did so.[40] A second study conducted by FDIC in 2007 surveyed individuals prior and subsequent to their participation in the program and also followed up by telephone 6 to 12 months after their final class. It found that participants were more likely to open deposit accounts, save money in a mainstream deposit product, use and adhere to a budget, and experience greater confidence in their

---

[38]The Urban Institute, *National Foreclosure Mitigation Counseling Program Evaluation: Final Report, Rounds 1 and 2* (Washington, D.C.: December 2011).

[39]When controlling for multiple factors, the study found that the course did not have an impact on most financial behaviors, with the exception that soldiers who took the course were more likely than the comparison group to report using informal spending plans and less likely to report using formal spending plans. The authors controlled for the following additional factors: years in the military, pay grade, gender, education, race/ethnicity, marital status, premilitary experiences, and possession of a credit card. Catherine Bell, Daniel Gorin, and Jeanne M. Hogarth, *Does Financial Education Affect Soldiers' Financial Behavior?* (Terre Haute, Ind.: Networks Financial Institute, August 2009).

[40]Angela Lyons and Erik Scherpf, *An Evaluation of the FDIC's Financial Literacy Program Money Smart* (University of Illinois at Urbana-Champaign, May 2003).

GAO-12-588 Federal Financial Literacy Programs

financial abilities.[41] However, this study did not have the benefit of a control group—that is, it did not measure participants in the program against a comparison group that did not participate in the program. FDIC is currently evaluating the effect of Money Smart for Young Adults on the financial knowledge and behavior of young adults (ages 12 to 20). The agency said it expects the evaluation to be completed by the end of 2013.

- *HUD housing counseling.* In 2008, HUD published a report that presented a systematic overview of the housing counseling industry and HUD-approved housing counseling providers.[42] In May 2012, two reports were published resulting from the Housing Counseling Outcome Evaluation. The first report looked at a sample of individuals who received foreclosure mitigation counseling from HUD-funded and HUD-approved agencies between August 2009 and December 2009.[43] The findings indicated that 18 months after initiating foreclosure counseling, 56 percent of homeowners were in the home and current on their payments, 28 percent were in the home and behind on their payments, and 16 percent were out of the home. However, the study did not include a control group to compare this group of homeowners to others who had not received foreclosure counseling. The second report examined prepurchase counseling and found that 35 percent of the study participants had become homeowners 18 months after seeking prepurchase counseling; this study also did not include a control group.[44] HUD is in the process of conducting an additional prepurchase counseling demonstration and impact evaluation that will track up to 6,000 individuals to examine the effectiveness of different housing counseling delivery methods

---

[41]Federal Deposit Insurance Corporation, *A Longitudinal Evaluation of the Intermediate-term Impact of the Money Smart Financial Education Curriculum upon Consumers' Behavior and Confidence* (Washington, D.C.: Apr. 2007).

[42]Christopher E. Herbert, Jennifer Turnham, and Christopher N. Rodger, *The State of the Housing Counseling Industry*, Abt Associates Inc. for the U.S. Department of Housing and Urban Development (Cambridge, Mass.: Sept. 2008).

[43]Anna Jefferson, Jonathan Spader, Jennifer Turnham, and Shawn Moulton, *Foreclosure Counseling Outcome Study: Final Report*, Abt Associates Inc. for the U.S. Department of Housing and Urban Development (Cambridge, Mass.: May 2012).

[44]Jennifer Turnham, and Anna Jefferson, *Pre-Purchase Counseling Outcome Study: Research Brief*, Abt Associates Inc. for the U.S. Department of Housing and Urban Development (Bethesda, Md.: May 2012).

compared to a control group of individuals not receiving counseling. Data collection is expected to begin around September 2012, and an initial report is expected by May 2014.

- *Financial Literacy Research Consortium.* In 2009 the Social Security Administration established a Financial Literacy Research Consortium that funded 63 research projects at three academic centers on a range of consumer financial behavior and retirement savings issues. According to agency staff, 11 of these projects included evaluations of the effectiveness of interventions designed to improve consumer financial literacy. For example, one study funded through the consortium at the University of Wisconsin found that a 5-hour online financial education module led to modest increases in knowledge of financial issues, but no changes in self-reported financial behaviors 3 months later.[45] Another project has randomly assigned 600 homebuyers to varying combinations of financial planning interventions to be completed during the first year after home purchase.[46] The project is ongoing, and evaluation of the effectiveness of the interventions will be conducted in subsequent years.[47]

- *U.S. Department of Agriculture Family and Consumer Economics programs.* The Department of Agriculture encourages land-grant institutions receiving grants for financial literacy activities to conduct some form of evaluation, and some grantees have sought to evaluate program outcomes. For example, researchers at Ohio State University examined the outcomes of a youth curriculum designed to enhance money management skills. Three months after the completion of the program, more than 80 percent of students in 6th-12th grades

---

[45]J. Michael Collins, *Online Financial Education for Employees: A Randomized Experiment* (University of Wisconsin, CFS Research Brief (*FLRC 11-13*): October 2011).

[46]Stephanie Moulton, Cäzilia Loibl, J. Michael Collins, and Anya Savikhin, *Field Experiments on the Impacts of Financial Planning Interventions for Recent Homebuyers*, University of Wisconsin Center for Financial Security Working Paper, October 2011.

[47]Although the Financial Literacy Consortium received no new funding after fiscal year 2010, the Social Security Administration allowed three grantees funded by the consortium to use grant funds until September 29, 2012, to complete their projects.

GAO-12-588 Federal Financial Literacy Programs

reported improvements in the extent to which they repaid money on time, set aside money for the future, and compared prices.[48]

- *Financial Education for College Access and Success Program.* In 2010, the U.S. Department of Education's Financial Education for College Access and Success Program provided a grant to the Tennessee Department of Education to measure the program's effect on student knowledge, attitudes, and behaviors, including rates of financial aid form completion, college enrollment, decisions regarding financial aid, and use of financial products and services. Agency officials said that the study will also measure the effect of the project on the knowledge, attitudes, and instructional skills of participating teachers. Results of the study were not available as of May 2012.

- *Financial Education and Counseling Pilot Program.* Treasury requires the homebuyer counseling organizations that receive program grants to periodically report on the results of two output goals (numbers served and hours of service provided) and three outcome goals chosen by the grantees (such as changes in participant savings, credit scores, or debt). As of April 2012, limited information was available about the program's impact because grantees had provided outcome data no earlier than 2011, while some of the desired outcomes of their programs can take years to realize.[49]

- *Wi$eUp.* As of 2010, more than 19,000 individuals had participated in Wi$eUp's eight-module financial education curriculum. The program tracks the percentage of participants who, as a result of their participation, reduced their debt and increased their savings or investments. Individuals complete pre- and postassessments for each module and are asked to complete a 3-month follow-up assessment to determine the financial changes they have made. Sixty-nine percent of participants in programs conducted in 2009 by Texas A&M's AgriLife Extension reported reducing their debt by a median of $500 since taking the Wi$eUp course, and 62 percent reported

---

[48]Lisa Sotak, Theresa M. Ferrari, Nancy W. Hudson, Graham Cochran, and Beth L. Bridgeman, *Outcomes of Participation in Real Money, Real World, 2007 Statewide Evaluation Final Report*, Ohio State University Extension, Mar. 17, 2008.

[49]For additional information on the program, see GAO, *Financial Education and Counseling Program,* GAO-11-737R (Washington, D.C.: July 27, 2011).

GAO-12-588 Federal Financial Literacy Programs

increasing their savings or investments.

Some agencies that we reviewed, while not assessing program effect on participant behavior, have reported on the effect on participant knowledge or attitudes or have future plans for evaluating behavior:

- *Excellence in Economic Education Program.* In 2009, program subgrantees gave standardized tests to 6,040 middle and high school students and 894 teachers shortly after they had completed the economics and personal finance instructional activities of the Excellence in Economic Education Program. Fifty-eight percent of students participating in projects funded through the program scored proficient on standardized tests of economics, personal finance, or both, compared to their target goal of 70 percent. In addition, 82 percent of teachers participating in the projects showed a significant increase in their scores on a standardized measure of economic content knowledge, as compared to the target goal of 70 percent.

- *Federal Reserve System.* Staff of the Board of Governors of the Federal Reserve System told us that the board does not conduct assessments of its financial literacy activities. However, some regional Federal Reserve Banks—which are part of the system but are not themselves federal agencies—do assess their own financial literacy activities. For example, the Federal Reserve Bank of Atlanta, in partnership with the Federal Reserve Bank of St. Louis, used third-party experts to conduct a 2-year assessment of the effectiveness of their financial literacy programs and materials, as well as to design and test tools for measuring knowledge gains and behavior changes.

- *DOD Family Support Centers.* DOD is in the second phase of the Military Family Life Project, a longitudinal department-wide survey of 40,000 married active-duty servicemembers and 100,000 military spouses designed to capture the long-term impact of deployment on families and to improve the support provided to them. According to DOD staff, one purpose of the study is to assess the financial readiness of servicemembers. In addition, DOD staff told us that as part of a larger evaluation effort of its family support programs, DOD is collaborating with a team of researchers from Pennsylvania State University to develop outcome measures for the department's financial readiness campaign and the services of its personal finance counselors. While the outcomes to be measured are still being determined, they may include changes in servicemembers' financial knowledge and behaviors, the staff said.

- *Consumer Financial Protection Bureau.* CFPB's financial literacy efforts have not been in place long enough for evaluation, but staff told us that evaluation will be a key component of its financial literacy activities and, as discussed later in this report, the bureau's Office of Financial Education contracted with a third party with specialized expertise to help assess the effectiveness of financial literacy programs.

Outcome-based evaluation is not always well suited for some financial literacy efforts, such as those that use mass media or distribute informational materials broadly. As such, several federal financial literacy programs that we reviewed collect information largely on output measures, such as number of individuals served or the volume of materials distributed. In some instances, the programs also measure the degree to which customers are satisfied with the service provided.

- *Federal Trade Commission.* FTC's Division of Consumer and Business Education tracks its financial literacy activities based on materials distributed and webpages accessed by consumers and businesses. It reported that in 2010 it distributed more than 17 million publications and its consumer and business education websites were accessed more than 26 million times.

- *Office of the Comptroller of the Currency.* The agency collects data on the number of website hits, media placements, audience reach, and the dollar value of donated air time for its public service announcements. In fiscal year 2011, it ran four media campaigns related to financial literacy, which included print and radio features in English and Spanish that appeared 14,079 times in 44 states. Its Consumer Education websites received 699,904 visits.

- *SEC Office of Investor Education and Advocacy.* SEC measures the number of investors its education efforts reach, which was 17.8 million in fiscal year 2010. SEC staff told us they are planning a future evaluation that will include, among other things, customer satisfaction with usefulness of investor education programs and materials. In addition, the Dodd-Frank Act directed SEC to submit by July 21, 2012, a study of retail investors' financial literacy, which must identify "the most effective existing private and public efforts to educate investors."

- *National Education and Resource Center on Women and Retirement Planning.* Staff at the Department of Health and Human Services told us they had not evaluated the program, but that the nonprofit administering the program had distributed more than 3,000 copies of publications and training materials available at conferences and workshops directed to the financial services industry, women's groups, advocacy groups, and senior centers.

- *Treasury's Office of Financial Access, Financial Education, and Consumer Protection.* The office collects participation statistics for its National Financial Capability Challenge, which provides teaching resources and encouragement and tests high school students on personal finance topics, and reported 84,372 students and 2,517 educators participating in 2011. The program also collects and publicly reports on average scores (by state and nationally), perfect scores, and students in the top 20 percent of scores nationally and by state.

- *Saving Matters Retirement Savings Education Campaign.* The Department of Labor conducts surveys at the program's seminars and webcasts as part of an in-house evaluation process. The evaluations, conducted with the assistance of the Gallup Organization, assess the number of participants reached by the program, usefulness of the program, and satisfaction of participants, with a goal of an 85 percent satisfaction rate on its seminars, workshops, and webcasts. The department also tracks attendance at these events, the distribution of its publications, and the use of interactive online tools, videos, and webcast archives.

Several Efforts to Better Assess Effectiveness Are Under Way

As discussed previously, several federal financial literacy programs—such as Money Smart for Young Adults, HUD's Housing Counseling Assistance Program, and the DOD Financial Readiness Campaign—are in the early stages of significant evaluations that may provide information about program effectiveness in the future. In addition to those evaluations of individual agency efforts, certain other federal efforts are under way that apply across agencies and seek more broadly to understand the most effective methods and strategies for improving financial literacy.[50]

- *Financial Literacy and Education Commission.* The 2011 national strategy and its implementation plan set as one of its four goals

---

[50]In GAO-12-342SP, we stated that we expected to recommend that Congress consider requiring federal agencies to evaluate the effectiveness of their financial literacy efforts. Based on our subsequent review of the measures described in this section, we believe that such a recommendation is not necessary at this time.

identifying, enhancing, and sharing effective practices. As previously discussed, Treasury staff told us that the commission has begun to establish a clearinghouse of evidence-based research and evaluation studies, current financial topics and trends of interest to consumers, innovative approaches, and best practices. According to Treasury staff, the clearinghouse will be available through the MyMoney.gov website and will have links to research and data sets from federally supported financial literacy projects. The clearinghouse is being developed by a contractor but will be maintained by Treasury and is expected to be available around September 2012. In addition, the commission's Research and Evaluation Working Group is charged with encouraging multidisciplinary research and sharing effective practices among federal agencies. In May 2012, the working group released a report on research questions and priorities that is intended to inform federal agencies, researchers, and others on the most important questions facing the field of financial literacy and to help make best use of limited research dollars.[51]

- *CFPB's Office of Financial Education.* CFPB's Office of Financial Education recently contracted with The Urban Institute for a financial education program evaluation project, which seeks to increase understanding of which interventions can improve financial decision-making skills in consumers. The effectiveness of selected financial education programs will be evaluated using a data collection tool and will be tested against a control group. Staff told us they intend to use the insights from the study to provide direction to practitioners about how to design and support effective financial capability and money confidence programs. A report is expected to be issued in the spring of 2014. In addition, CFPB's Office of Financial Education has collaborated with its Office of Research to develop metrics for financial education, according to agency staff.

- *Office of Personnel Management.* As part of its Retirement Readiness NOW program, the Office of Personnel Management is developing a rating system to determine which federal agencies are most effective in providing financial literacy and retirement education to the civilian labor force. According to agency staff, the ranking system is intended to help hold federal agencies accountable for their retirement

---

[51]Financial Literacy and Education Commission, *2012 Research Priorities and Research Questions: Financial Literacy and Education Commission Research & Evaluation Working Group* (Washington, D.C.: May 2012).

education plans and strategies.

- *Treasury's Office of Financial Access, Financial Education, and Consumer Protection.* This office has contracted out a research project assessing financial capability outcomes for both youth and adults, with results expected by the end of 2012. The office will test the hypothesis that increased financial capability—including financial information and education and access to simple, low-cost, transaction and savings products—will enhance the financial stability and well-being of low- and moderate-income individuals and households.

Conclusions

Federal financial literacy and housing counseling resources are spread across many federal agencies, the result of both legislation and programs evolving to address a variety of populations or topics. While we uncovered no duplication, some agencies or programs do have overlapping goals and activities, which raises the risk of inefficiency and underscores the importance of coordination. The creation of CFPB adds a new player to the mix. The agency will play a primary federal role in addressing financial literacy, yet some of its responsibilities overlap with those of other federal agencies. Effective collaboration among agencies entails defining and agreeing on respective roles and responsibilities and organizing collective efforts. CFPB appears to be making progress thus far in coordinating with federal agencies that have overlapping financial literacy responsibilities, but ensuring clear delineation of respective roles and responsibilities will also be essential to ensure efficiency. Moreover, the creation of CFPB may signal an opportunity for reconsidering how the federal government's financial literacy efforts are organized. In particular, some consolidation of these efforts could help ensure the most efficient and effective use of federal financial literacy resources. While our February 2012 report stated that we expected to suggest that Congress consider options for such consolidation, the Financial Literacy and Education Commission is better positioned to identify possible options and this would be consistent with the commission's statutory responsibility to propose means of eliminating overlap and duplication among federal financial literacy activities.

Overall, coordination among federal agencies with regard to financial literacy has improved in recent years, and the commission has played a critical role in this. The commission's 2011 national strategy includes some elements that may be useful in guiding federal financial literacy efforts, but it could do more to identify the resources needed to implement the strategy and how federal resources might best be allocated among programs and agencies, characteristics we have found to be desirable for any national strategy. The commission faces the constraints of lacking its own budget or legal authority over member agencies to take any action, but, even so, it has the ability to provide recommendations or guidance to Congress or federal agencies. Without a clear discussion of resource needs and where resources should be targeted, policymakers lack information to help direct the strategy's implementation and help ensure efficient use of funds.

We found that nearly all significant federal financial literacy programs that we reviewed had assessed or measured their activities in some manner and many had undertaken some method of seeking to measure outcomes. While some measured the effect on participant behavior, often they assessed changes in participant knowledge or tracked output measures, such as the number of consumers reached. There is only limited knowledge about which federal financial literacy programs are most effective in achieving the key goal of improving consumer behavior, in large part because of the cost and difficulty of measuring these outcomes. Rigorous outcome-based evaluation is not necessarily practical or appropriate for every program, but its promotion and use, where feasible, is important to help Congress and federal agencies focus financial literacy resources on the most effective approaches and activities. In our February 2012 report, we stated that we expected to recommend that Congress consider requiring federal agencies to evaluate the effectiveness of their financial literacy efforts. However, we have found that the new initiatives that CFPB, Treasury, and the Financial Literacy and Education Commission have under way to assess effectiveness and identify best practices are positive steps in this direction. As a result, based on these ongoing efforts, we no longer believe that this recommendation is necessary at this time.

Recommendations for Executive Action

We recommend that as part of its ongoing coordination efforts, the Consumer Financial Protection Bureau take steps to help ensure clear delineation of the respective roles and responsibilities between itself and other federal agencies that have overlapping financial literacy responsibilities.

To help ensure effective and efficient use of federal financial literacy resources, we also recommend that the Secretary of the Treasury and the Director of the Consumer Financial Protection Bureau, in their capacity as Chair and Vice Chair of the Financial Literacy and Education

Commission, and in concert with other agency representatives of the commission:

- identify for federal agencies and Congress options for consolidating federal financial literacy efforts into the activities and agencies that are best suited or most effective, and

- revise the commission's national strategy to incorporate clear recommendations on the allocation of federal financial literacy resources across programs and agencies.

Agency Comments and Our Evaluation

We provided a draft of this report to the Departments of Agriculture, Defense, Education, Health and Human Services, Housing and Urban Development, Labor, and the Treasury, as well as to the Board of Governors of the Federal Reserve System, Consumer Financial Protection Bureau, Federal Deposit Insurance Corporation, Federal Trade Commission, Office of the Comptroller of the Currency, Office of Personnel Management, Securities and Exchange Commission, and the Social Security Administration. We incorporated technical comments provided by these agencies as appropriate. In addition, CFPB, the Department of Health and Human Services, and Treasury provided written responses that are reproduced in appendices III, IV, and V, respectively.

In its response, CFPB neither agreed nor disagreed with the recommendations addressed to it, but it highlighted steps that its Offices of Financial Education, Servicemember Affairs, and Financial Protection for Older Americans are taking to delineate roles and responsibilities, improve coordination, and avoid duplication with other federal agencies. CFPB also noted that it is committed to ensuring that its activities are informed by data and analytics. For example, it cited a project it has launched that uses rigorous quantitative methodologies to assess the effectiveness of several existing financial education programs and provide direction to practitioners about how to design and support effective programs on improving consumers' financial capability and confidence about money.

Treasury said that it agreed with our recommendations to the Financial Literacy and Education Commission related to identifying options for consolidation and making recommendations on the allocation of federal financial literacy resources. Treasury noted that the department has already begun work with other members of the commission to define specific and measurable objectives that will help agencies assess the impact of their financial capability activities, which will provide a framework for any resource allocation recommendations the commission may have.

The Department of Health and Human Services said in its response that it disagreed that its National Education and Resource Center on Women and Retirement Planning overlapped with the Department of Labor's Wi$eUp program because the two programs have differing methodologies, approaches, and target populations. We acknowledge the differences between the two programs in our report. However, the definition for overlap presented in this report is "multiple agencies or programs with similar goals and activities," and we believe that this accurately applies to these two programs, both of which are financial literacy programs designed for adult women.

We are sending copies of this report to the appropriate congressional committees and to the heads of agencies that comprise the Financial Literacy and Education Commission. In addition, the report will be available at no charge on the GAO website at http://www.gao.gov.

If you or your staff have any questions concerning this report, please contact me at (202) 512-8678 or cackleya@gao.gov. Contact points for our Offices of Congressional Relations and Public Affairs may be found on the last page of this report. GAO staff who made major contributions are listed in appendix VI.

Alicia Puente Cackley
Director, Financial Markets and Community Investment

Appendix I: Objectives, Scope, and Methodology

Our objectives were to address (1) what is known about the cost of federal financial literacy activities; (2) the extent and consequences of overlap and fragmentation among financial literacy activities; (3) what the federal government is doing to coordinate its financial literacy activities; and (4) what is known about the effectiveness of federal financial literacy activities. For the purposes of our analysis, we considered duplication to occur when two or more agencies or programs are engaged in the same activities and provide the same services to the same beneficiaries. Overlap refers to when multiple agencies or programs have similar goals, engage in similar activities or strategies to achieve them, or target similar users. Fragmentation refers to circumstances in which more than one federal agency is involved in the same broad area of national need. Our report focuses largely on federal programs or activities that were relatively comprehensive in scope or scale and included financial literacy as a key component rather than a tangential goal. We generally excluded from our review programs or activities for which financial literacy was only a minimal component; that provided financial information related to the administration of the program itself rather than information aimed at increasing the beneficiaries' financial literacy and comprehension more generally; that were purely internal to the agency; or that provided individualized financial services or advice rather than education. Using these criteria, we identified 16 significant financial literacy programs and 4 significant housing counseling programs in operation in fiscal year 2010.

To address our first objective, we collected and reviewed the President's Budget for fiscal years 2010, 2012, and 2013; budget justifications, as needed; congressional appropriations; and other sources that included cost information. For many federal agencies, financial literacy activities were not organized as separate budget line items or cost centers. In these cases, we asked agency staff to estimate the portion of program costs that could be attributed to financial literacy activities for fiscal year 2010, which is the year for which we reported costs. This typically entailed estimating the cost of that portion of staff time devoted to financial literacy, as well as the cost of contracts, printing, or other resources related to financial literacy activities. Because the methods for estimating costs varied, these costs may not be fully comparable across agencies. To assess the reliability of these estimates, we interviewed agency staff about their cost estimation methodology, what their estimate included, and what assumptions they used in making the estimate. Although costs may not be comparable across the agencies because agencies used differing methodologies, we determined that the data are reliable for the purposes of generally estimating federal dollars spent on financial literacy activities.

To address our second and third objectives, we reviewed a 2009 report
by the RAND Corporation that cataloged federal financial literacy efforts;
reports from the President's Advisory Council on Financial Capability; the
national strategies and supporting documents of the Financial Literacy
and Education Commission; and other reports as appropriate. We also
reviewed the commission's MyMoney.gov website and the websites of
individual federal agencies related to financial literacy. In addition, we
reviewed federal agency strategic plans; performance and accountability
reports; budget justifications; memorandums of understanding between
agencies or with nonfederal entities; and laws related to financial literacy
activities or programs. Further, to assess the extent of overlap or
duplication, we collected and analyzed characteristics of federal financial
literacy programs and identified similarities and differences among
programs' purposes, subject matter content, targeted populations, and
delivery methods. We assessed the commission's 2011 National Strategy
for Financial Literacy, in part, by benchmarking it against our prior work
that identified the general characteristics of an effective national strategy.[1]

Those recommended characteristics for national strategies had been
developed by reviewing several sources of information, which included
the Government Performance and Results Act of 1993; legislative and
executive branch guidance for national strategies; general literature on
strategic planning and performance; and our prior work on issues related
to planning, integration, implementation, and other related subjects.

To determine what is known about the effectiveness of federal financial
literacy activities, we collected evaluations, as well as any available
information on the outputs or outcomes of these activities. As applicable,
we reviewed output data such as information on numbers of program
participants or consumers reached, website visits, and copies of
publications or other materials distributed that were available through a
variety of sources. For example, as available, we reviewed results of
surveys of customer satisfaction, attitudes, or intention to change
behavior, and tests that measured changes in program participants'
knowledge. In addition, we reviewed information on program effect that
appeared in agencies' strategic plans and performance and accountability
reports. We also reviewed the 2009 RAND report, which included self-
reported information from federal agencies on methods they have used to
evaluate their financial literacy programs, and we updated this information

---

[1]GAO-04-408T and GAO-07-100.

as necessary through interviews with agency staff. In addition, we collected any available studies and evaluations that had been conducted on the outcomes of federal financial literacy activities, which included evaluations conducted by the agencies themselves or by external researchers. Each of the studies and evaluations cited in our report was reviewed for methodological reliability and determined to be sufficiently reliable for our purposes.

Finally, to address all four of our objectives, we interviewed staff who address financial literacy issues at 17 federal agencies that we had identified in prior work as potentially having significant involvement in financial literacy—the Board of Governors of the Federal Reserve System; Consumer Financial Protection Bureau; Departments of Agriculture, Defense, Education, Health and Human Services, Housing and Urban Development, Labor, and Treasury; Federal Deposit Insurance Corporation; Federal Trade Commission; Internal Revenue Service; Office of the Comptroller of the Currency; Office of Personnel Management; Securities and Exchange Commission; Social Security Administration; and the U.S. Mint. We also interviewed staff at NeighborWorks America (a federally chartered nonprofit corporation) and representatives of the National Financial Education Network of State and Local Governments, the President's Advisory Council on Financial Capability, and two nonprofit organizations, the American Savings Education Council and the National Endowment for Financial Education.

We conducted this performance audit from May 2011 to July 2012 in accordance with generally accepted government auditing standards. Those standards require that we plan and perform the audit to obtain sufficient, appropriate evidence to provide a reasonable basis for our findings and conclusions based on our audit objectives. We believe that the evidence obtained provides a reasonable basis for our findings and conclusions based on our audit objectives.

Appendix II: Crosswalk between Federal Financial Literacy Programs Identified in the RAND Report and Programs Selected for Inclusion in this Report

In 2009, the Departments of the Treasury and Education asked federal agencies to self-identify their financial literacy efforts, which resulted in a 2009 report by the RAND Corporation that identified 56 federal financial literacy programs among 20 agencies.[1] We reported these results in a 2011 report, but our subsequent analysis of these 56 programs found a high degree of inconsistency in how different agencies defined financial literacy programs or efforts and whether they counted related efforts as one or multiple programs.[2] For the purposes of our current report, we developed criteria for identifying significant federal financial literacy and housing counseling activities and programs. We defined such activities or programs as those that were relatively comprehensive in scope or scale and for which financial literacy or housing counseling was a key objective rather than a tangential goal. As appropriate, we defined a related set of activities (such as a series of webpages from one agency) as a single program. In addition, we excluded programs or activities (1) for which financial literacy was only a minimal component; (2) that provided financial information related to the administration of the program itself rather that information aimed at increasing the beneficiaries' financial literacy and comprehension more generally; (3) that were purely internal to the agency, such as information provided to agency employees on their employment and retirement benefits; and (4) that represented individualized services or advice. We included as federal programs those of NeighborWorks America, a government-chartered, nonprofit corporation that receives federal funding for housing counseling, including through an annual appropriation from Congress. Finally, the RAND report was based on programs and activities in place in 2009, while our list reflects programs and activities in place during fiscal year 2010.

---

[1]Angela A. Hung, Kata Mihaly, and Joanne K. Yoong (RAND Corporation), "Federal Financial and Economic Literacy Education Programs, 2009" (Santa Monica, Calif.: 2010). http://www.rand.org/content/dam/rand/pubs/technical_reports/2010/RAND_TR857.pdf.

[2]GAO-11-318SP.

Appendix II: Crosswalk between Federal
Financial Literacy Programs Identified in the
RAND Report and Programs Selected for
Inclusion in this Report

Figure 1: Crosswalk between Federal Financial Literacy Programs Identified in the RAND Report and Programs Selected for Inclusion in This Report (GAO-12-588)

Agency	Programs identified in 2009 RAND report		Programs and activities cited in this report (GAO-12-588)
Consumer Financial Protection Bureau			1. Office of Financial Education and other offices
Commodity Futures Trading Commission	1. www.cftc.gov	●	
Department of Agriculture	2. Financial Security Program		2. Family and Consumer Economics programs
Department of Defense	3. Financial Readiness Campaign		3. Personal Financial Management Program (located within Family Support Centers)
Department of Education	4. Cooperative Civic Education and Economic Exchange Program	●	
	5. Excellence in Economic Education Program		4. Excellence in Economic Education Program
			5. Financial Education for College Access and Success Program
Department of Health and Human Services	6. Own Your Future Long-Term Care Awareness Campaign	●	
	7. National Education and Resource Center on Women and Retirement Planning		6. National Education and Resource Center on Women and Retirement Planning
	8. Pension Counseling and Information Program	▲	
	9. Aging and Disability Resource Center	●★	
	10. Medicare Improvements for Patients and Providers Act	●★	
	11. Medicaid Program Eligibility	●★	
	12. Medicare Options Compare	●★	
	13. Medicare Prescription Drug Plan Finder	●★	
	14. Insure Kids Now Hotline and Website	●★	
	15. Questions and Answers about Health Insurance: A Consumer Guide	●	
	16. Executive Leadership Development Program	●	
	17. Public Health Officer Basic Course	■	
	18. Pre-Retirement Seminar	■	

Reasons that program or activity does not fall within the scope of this engagement:

● Financial literacy was a minimal component
★ Related to administration of program
■ Employee benefits--internal to agency
✖ Discontinued after 2009
▲ Individualized services or advice

Graphic continued on next page.

Agency	Programs identified in 2009 RAND report		Programs and activities cited in this report (GAO-12-588)
Department of Housing and Urban Development	19. Housing Counseling		7. Housing Counseling Assistance Program
Department of Labor	20. Saving Matters Retirement Savings Education Campaign		8. Savings Matters Retirement Savings Education Campaign
	21. Wi$eUp		9. Wi$eUp
	22. Health Benefits Education Campaign	●	
Department of the Treasury	23. National Financial Capability Challenge		10. Office of Financial Education and Financial Access
	24. Money Math: Lessons for Life		10. Office of Financial Education and Financial Access
	25. Financial Education and Counseling Pilot Program		11. Financial Education and Counseling Pilot Program
	26. Community Financial Access Pilot	✖	
Department of Veterans Affairs	27. Financial Literacy Education Program	■	
Federal Deposit Insurance Corporation	28. Money Smart Financial Education Program		12. Money Smart Financial Education Program
	29. FDIC Consumer Protection Resources	●	
	30. FDIC Deposit Insurance Coverage Resources	●★	
Federal Reserve Board	31. Financial education initiatives		13. Division of Consumer and Community Affairs and Office of Public Affairs
Federal Trade Commission	32. Ftc.gov/moneymatters		14. Division of Consumer and Business Education
	33. Ftc.gov/freereports		14. Division of Consumer and Business Education
	34. Ftc.gov/youarehere		14. Division of Consumer and Business Education
	35. Ftc.gov/gettingcredit		14. Division of Consumer and Business Education
	36. Youtube.com/ftcvideos		14. Division of Consumer and Business Education
	37. Ftc.gov/idtheft		14. Division of Consumer and Business Education
	38. Ftc.gov/bizopps		14. Division of Consumer and Business Education
	39. Ftc.gov/hurricanerecovery		14. Division of Consumer and Business Education
U.S. Mint	40. Mint Education Initiative	●	
National Credit Union Association	41. Deposit Insurance Education Campaign	●★	

Reasons that program or activity does not fall within the scope of this engagement:

- ● Financial literacy was a minimal component
- ★ Related to administration of program
- ■ Employee benefits--internal to agency
- ✖ Discontinued after 2009
- ▲ Individualized services or advice

Graphic continued on next page.

Appendix II: Crosswalk between Federal
Financial Literacy Programs Identified in the
RAND Report and Programs Selected for
Inclusion in this Report

Agency	Programs identified in 2009 RAND report	Programs and activities cited in this report (GAO-12-588)
Office of the Comptroller of the Currency	42. helpwithmybank.gov	
	43. Consumer Advisories	
	44. Public Service Announcements	
	45. Minority Media Campaign	
	46. Financial Literacy Web Resource Directory	15. Consumer education activities
	47. Financial Literacy Update	
	48. Other Financial Literacy Publications	
	49. OCC Staff Support and Consumer Information	
	50. OCC Leadership and Support	
	51. Federal Regulations and Policies That Impact Financial Literacy, Particularly the Community Reinvestment Act	
Office of Personnel Management	52. Retirement Readiness NOW	16. Retirement Readiness NOW
Securities and Exchange Commission	53. Office of Investor Education and Advocacy	17. Office of Investor Education and Advocacy
Small Business Administration	54. Financial Literacy Resource Directory ●	
Social Security Administration	55. SSA Special Initiative to Encourage Saving	18. Financial Literacy Research Consortium
Financial Literacy and Education Commission	56. Mymoney.gov	Now under Treasury (#10 in this column)
NeighborWorks America		19. National Foreclosure Mitigation Counseling Program
		20. Other housing counseling activities

Reasons that program or activity does not
fall within the scope of this engagement:

● Financial literacy was a minimal component
★ Related to administration of program
■ Employee benefits--internal to agency
✖ Discontinued after 2009
▲ Individualized services or advice

Source: GAO analysis of federal financial literacy programs and activities and Angela A. Hung, Kata Mihaly, and Joanne K. Yoong (RAND Corporation), "Federal Financial and Economic Literacy Education Programs, 2009" (Santa Monica, Calif.: 2010).

July 3, 2012

Ms. Alicia Cackley
Director
Financial Markets and Community Investment
Government Accountability Office
441 G Street, NW
Washington, DC 20548

Dear Ms. Cackley:

This letter responds to the request by the Government Accountability Office (GAO) that the Consumer Financial Protection Bureau (the "Bureau" or the CFPB) comment on Financial Literacy: Overlap of Programs Suggests There May Be Opportunities for Consolidation, GAO-12-588.

We appreciate the opportunity to provide comments pertaining to the activities of the CFPB's Offices of Financial Education (OFE), Servicemember Affairs, and Financial Protection for Older Americans.

We agree with the finding that "GAO has not identified duplication" among federal financial literacy and housing counseling activities. Federal agencies involved in financial education have different missions, regulatory authorities, constituencies, and expertise. The CFPB is the only federal agency whose primary focus and mandate is the protection and education of the American financial consumer. The Bureau's statutory function to provide consumers with accessible information about financial products, services, and decisions creates an enormous opportunity to reach consumers at the right moment with targeted information that can increase their financial management skills and money confidence.

Our Offices of Financial Education, Servicemember Affairs, and Older Americans are engaged in initiatives that advance financial education opportunities for American families in a manner that leverages and complements existing federal efforts. By meaningfully engaging with other agencies, including Financial Literacy and Education Commission (FLEC) partners, we work to delineate roles and responsibilities, to improve coordination, and avoid duplication while working to execute on our statutorily mandated responsibilities to educate and empower consumers to make informed financial decisions. CFPB's Director serves as the Vice-Chairman of the Financial Literacy and Education Commission. OFE staff meets regularly with the Department of the Treasury staff members in the Office of Financial Education and Financial Access to ensure coordination.

The Office of Servicemember Affairs, under the leadership of Holly Petraeus, works in partnership with the Department of Defense (DoD) to ensure that military personnel and families receive the financial education they need to make financial decisions best suited to their particular circumstances. A key component of the Office of Servicemember Affairs' direction is to identify opportunities to make improvements on existing efforts and to avoid duplication across agencies.

The CFPB's Office for Older Americans is the only federal office specifically focused on the financial health of seniors. Under the Director of Skip Humphrey, the Office works to provide older Americans and their caregivers the financial information they need to make informed financial decisions. In order to avoid duplication and maximize limited resources the Office for Older Americans works closely with federal agencies, state and local government entities, and community based-organizations to educate and protect seniors.

The CFPB is committed to ensuring that its activities are informed by data and analytics. As part of that effort, CFPB's Office of Financial Education has launched its initial Financial Education Program Evaluation Project. Using rigorous quantitative methodologies, this project will assess the effectiveness of several existing financial education programs to identify which program elements do or do not increase consumers' money confidence, and why. We intend to use the insights from this study to provide direction to practitioners about how to design and support effective financial capability and money confidence programs. The results will be widely shared with participating FLEC agencies and other relevant stakeholders. As the research project proceeds, we will also facilitate the sharing of programmatic best practices, evaluation methodologies, and common metrics that promote effective financial education among practitioners and other researchers.

2

consumerfinance.gov

The complex financial marketplace creates special challenges for
consumers and requires a range of strategies and approaches. We are
committed to thoughtfully focusing the talent of the Bureau on ensuring
that American families understand the choices available to them as they
manage their finances. We are equally committed to continuing our work
with federal agency partners to leverage all available resources, expertise,
and opportunities for improving the financial well-being of consumers.

We appreciate the opportunity to comment on this GAO report and we
look forward to continuing to work with you on enhancing the money
confidence and financial management skills of American consumers.

Sincerely,

Camille M. Busette, PhD

Assistant Director

Office of Financial Education

consumerfinance.gov

3

Appendix IV: Comments from the Department of Health and Human Services

 DEPARTMENT OF HEALTH & HUMAN SERVICES

OFFICE OF THE SECRETARY

Assistant Secretary for Legislation
Washington, DC 20201

JUN 26 2012

Alicia Puente Cackley, Director
Financial Records and Community Investment
U.S. Government Accountability Office
441 G Street NW
Washington, DC 20548

Dear Ms. Cackley:

Attached are comments on the U.S. Government Accountability Office's (GAO) report entitled, "Financial Literacy: Overlap of Programs Suggests There May Be Opportunities for Consolidation" (GAO-12-588).

The Department appreciates the opportunity to review this draft section of the report prior to publication.

Sincerely,

Jim R. Esquea
Assistant Secretary for Legislation

Attachment

**GENERAL COMMENTS OF THE DEPARTMENT OF HEALTH AND HUMAN
SERVICES (HHS) ON THE GOVERNMENT ACCOUNTABILITY OFFICE'S (GAO)
DRAFT REPORT ENTITLED, "FINANCIAL LITERACY: OVERLAP OF PROGRAMS
SUGGESTS THERE MAY BE OPPORTUNITIES FOR CONSOLIDATION" (GAO-12-
588)**

The Department appreciates the opportunity to comment on this draft report.

The report states that overlap can be found in two federal financial literacy programs designed
specifically for women – The Department of Labor's Wi$eup program and HHS's National
Education and Resource Center on Women and Retirement Planning. We do not believe there is
duplication or overlap between these programs for two reasons: 1) They have different
methodologies and approaches; and 2) They are targeted at different populations.

Differing methodologies

HHS's National Education and Resource Center on Women and Retirement Planning utilizes a
"train the trainer" approach, which utilizes peer counselors in the community providing
individual assistance to the targeted population. The Department of Labor's Wi$eup program
utilizes a webinar-based approach.

Different Target Populations

More importantly, the target population and goal of HHS's National Education and Resource
Center on Women and Retirement Planning is to address the financial literacy needs of low
income women, women of color, and women with limited English proficiency, while the purpose
of the Department of Labor's Wi$eup program is for more general informational purposes. This
distinction between the programs is significant. Results of a study by Annamaria Lusardi found
women experience a higher rate of financial illiteracy than men, and that education programs
targeted specifically at women may be better suited to addressing differences in financial
knowledge.[1] While, traditionally, the financial services industry had been reluctant to reach out
to women of all socioeconomic classes, it generally ignored low income women and women of
color. Specifically, the HHS Center:

- Serves as a trusted source for information by helping women make the best decisions
  they can with the limited resources they may have;

- Trains peer trainers who assist women in their communities and partners with
  organizations who work directly with women most at-risk;

- Assists the Aging Network of 56 State and 600 plus Area Agencies on Aging by
  providing information and resources to help more at-risk women stay in their homes,

---

[1] Lusardi, Annamaria, "Planning and Financial Literacy: How Do Women Fare?" 2006 Retirement
Research Center, University of Michigan, Ann Arbor, MI.

1

<u>**GENERAL COMMENTS OF THE DEPARTMENT OF HEALTH AND HUMAN
SERVICES (HHS) ON THE GOVERNMENT ACCOUNTABILITY OFFICE'S (GAO)
DRAFT REPORT ENTITLED, "FINANCIAL LITERACY: OVERLAP OF PROGRAMS
SUGGESTS THERE MAY BE OPPORTUNITIES FOR CONSOLIDATION" (GAO-12-
588)**</u>

avoid poverty, and reduce their likelihood of becoming overly dependent on government
programs;

- Develops targeted financial education for distinct populations of aging, caregiving and
  minority communities, including low-income women, women with limited English-
  speaking proficiencies and women who are divorced and widowed– women who
  traditionally have not had access to good financial planning information;

- Provides partners access to programs and information on strategies to reach vulnerable
  populations; and

- Reaches target populations through innovative interventions including a state-of-the-art
  technological clearinghouse through which all women can easily access educational
  materials and planning tools.

2

Appendix V: Comments from the Department of the Treasury

DEPARTMENT OF THE TREASURY
WASHINGTON, D.C. 20220

July 9, 2012

Alicia Cackley
Director, Financial Markets and Community Investments
Government Accountability Office

Dear Ms. Cackley:

Thank you for the opportunity to review and provide comments on the draft Government Accountability Office (GAO) report, *Financial Literacy: Overlap of Programs Suggests There May Be Opportunities for Consolidation.* The Department of the Treasury (Department) welcomes the GAO's ongoing interest in financial literacy and capability. The Secretary of the Treasury, as Chairperson of the Financial Literacy and Education Commission (Commission), is committed to promoting coordination among federal agencies and to increasing efficiencies in federal efforts in the area of financial education.

The Department agrees that the Commission should recommend ways to improve outcomes of the federal government's financial literacy efforts and allocate resources effectively across federal programs and agencies, such as by identifying options for consolidating overlapping programs and activities. To that end, the Department has begun work with other members of the Commission to define specific and measurable objectives that will help agencies assess the impact of their financial capability activities. This effort will be incorporated into the National Strategy for Financial Literacy through the Commission's next annual Strategy for Assuring Financial Empowerment report. We anticipate that this work will provide a framework for the Commission's resource allocation recommendations, if any. As reflected in the Commission's recently published 2012 Research Priorities and Research Questions, the Commission believes that federal investments in financial capability should be rooted in evidence of effectiveness.

As described in the draft GAO report, as part of our strategy to better enable coordination, avoid duplication and assess effectiveness, the Commission will develop a research clearinghouse on the MyMoney.gov website, which will enable researchers to share their research and data on financial education and related topics. This tool will allow for greater collaboration and avoidance of duplication in research and evaluation. The clearinghouse should be available by September 2012.

Thank you for your attention to the area of financial literacy and capability. We look forward to continued collaboration with your office on these topics.

Sincerely,

Melissa Koide
Deputy Assistant Secretary
Office of Financial Access, Financial Education and Consumer Protection

Appendix VI: GAO Contact and Staff Acknowledgments

GAO Contact	Alicia Puente Cackley, 202-512-8678 or cackleya@gao.gov
Staff Acknowledgments	In addition to the contact named above, Jason Bromberg (Assistant Director), Kimberly Cutright, Mary Coyle, Jonathan Kucskar, Roberto Piñero, Rhonda Rose, Jennifer Schwartz, and Andrew Stavisky made key contributions to this report.

GAO's Mission	The Government Accountability Office, the audit, evaluation, and investigative arm of Congress, exists to support Congress in meeting its constitutional responsibilities and to help improve the performance and accountability of the federal government for the American people. GAO examines the use of public funds; evaluates federal programs and policies; and provides analyses, recommendations, and other assistance to help Congress make informed oversight, policy, and funding decisions. GAO's commitment to good government is reflected in its core values of accountability, integrity, and reliability.
Obtaining Copies of GAO Reports and Testimony	The fastest and easiest way to obtain copies of GAO documents at no cost is through GAO's website (www.gao.gov). Each weekday afternoon, GAO posts on its website newly released reports, testimony, and correspondence. To have GAO e-mail you a list of newly posted products, go to www.gao.gov and select "E-mail Updates."
Order by Phone	The price of each GAO publication reflects GAO's actual cost of production and distribution and depends on the number of pages in the publication and whether the publication is printed in color or black and white. Pricing and ordering information is posted on GAO's website, http://www.gao.gov/ordering.htm. Place orders by calling (202) 512-6000, toll free (866) 801-7077, or TDD (202) 512-2537. Orders may be paid for using American Express, Discover Card, MasterCard, Visa, check, or money order. Call for additional information.
Connect with GAO	Connect with GAO on Facebook, Flickr, Twitter, and YouTube. Subscribe to our RSS Feeds or E-mail Updates. Listen to our Podcasts. Visit GAO on the web at www.gao.gov.
To Report Fraud, Waste, and Abuse in Federal Programs	Contact: Website: www.gao.gov/fraudnet/fraudnet.htm E-mail: fraudnet@gao.gov Automated answering system: (800) 424-5454 or (202) 512-7470
Congressional Relations	Katherine Siggerud, Managing Director, siggerudk@gao.gov, (202) 512-4400, U.S. Government Accountability Office, 441 G Street NW, Room 7125, Washington, DC 20548
Public Affairs	Chuck Young, Managing Director, youngc1@gao.gov, (202) 512-4800 U.S. Government Accountability Office, 441 G Street NW, Room 7149 Washington, DC 20548

www.ingramcontent.com/pod-product-compliance
Lightning Source LLC
Chambersburg PA
CBHW082244310526
45795CB00014B/2413